Emotional Feelings

Simulacradelic Press
Atlanta, GA
simulacradelicpress@gmail.com
www.simulacradelic.com

Cover & Design by Seth Stubbs
Edited by Seth Stubbs

Library of Congress Control Number: 2018932733
ISBN-13: 978-0-9993980-4-3 (PBK)
1. Poetry 2. Philosophy

First Edition

10 9 8 7 6 5 4 3 2 1

Printed in the United States of America

Emotional Feelings

Poems February 2016-August 2017

Ariel Samuel Ackrum

A: You're not doing shit.
B: I'm leaving the world to its own devices.
A: You're a piece of shit.
B: Obviously! I'm not *doing me*! Extroverted self-images like you fuck and shit themselves.

Emotional Feelings

Only the obliging redundancy of lovers can overcome the total,
systematic violence of compatibility.

1. Wisdom

When I discover wisdom,
I think about being afraid—
as I might have discovered it too young
and God might take my life.

I try to be clever
and deny I have wisdom
by putting it into tongues (poetry),
but then I remember that tongues
is what the Devil cannot interpret
(while God understands everything
because He had a hand in making it—
in the sense of 'the minute hand').

People loathe God like they loathed Jesus.
But I think God is just misunderstood.
I think he might, like X used to,
turn people away through truly ridiculous behavior
to see who'll return and be a homie.

I'm too young to know what I know.
The punishment for knowledge is death.
But was mortality *really* a punishment?
God's love is mysterious,
and we are either too young
or have gotten too old to understand it.
Probably a little of both,
since God is either old as fuck,
too young to be as effective as He is
or a woman (but NOT Alanis Morrissette,
for whatever reason).
He punished the immortal pair
with multiplicity and history.
It was immediate knowledge that God punished—
but as a master 'punishes' his initiate with hard labor—
with time.

The Devil wants to seduce without being seduced—
and *really believes* that he produces himself,
having forgotten his false consciousness.
He trips over his own shoelaces that he didn't tie
and blames Being.
The Devil hates Being—
who wouldn't appease him
with his own realm of ridicule
that doesn't know it is ridicule.

God might kill me for saying this,
but *resentment is hatred of seduction.*

The Devil produces to produce seduction.
God seduces for no reason at all,
not even to seduce production—
for what would be seductive about that?

2. Gifts

The gifts you receive from me are my leftovers.
You will never go hungry with me
because there is always something I didn't finish.
I will always have leftovers for you, my loves.

There are already men in abundance
who have become richer than they were
because of the women I have caught and released.

God is in the future, my loves.
Time only continues to pass
because He has already seen it all
and has grown bored of it all
so we get all those leftovers
that have had time to soak up their own juices
and soften for our chewing pleasure.

Thank God for boredom,
or else there'd be nothing left *for us*.

Accept these hand-me-downs,
and above all—outgrow them!
If my seductions bug you,
they will at least be courteous enough
to prevent a full-on infection with them.

Or else, my loves,
I will bask in the cruelty my seductiveness throws
upon your prudish judgements.

3. Simulators

America, whose politics is aesthetics,
made bourbon, the best whiskey for immoral drinkers
(scotch is as pretentious as wine with its formalism;
men learn about and argue over scotch).
The invention of bourbon made it possible
that the Irish didn't invent whiskey.

Forms can become unencumbered by substance.
America formulates questions *that it is*—
while Europe is always trying to find answers.
America embeds itself in the question
and the answers just come on their own accord—
and the answer is: *America*.
America, ending in the plural *a* (as in dejecta),
is never a State—it has always been a *form*.
And the Europeans are still imagining it's a property
(since they invented the imagination,
which we have also been able to produce more cheaply
and quickly)—
and properties are just habits that can be unlearned.

Simulators tend to be good at everything they do.
They also tend not to get caught up in authenticity—
since simulation is the authentic inauthentic.
But simulators are no less *real*
than the authenticity-obsessed peoples—
just like skeptics don't wander off cliffs
because they don't belief cliffs exist.

Presupposing the goal to be always-already achieved
in the initial (or initiatory) action
(since that action, too, is an effect),
the goal always follows—

and what a pleasure it is to be right
when you don't even believe in right.

4. Sufferers' logic

1. If I continue to suffer, God will have mercy on me.

2. God is too vain to destroy what he doesn't acknowledge.

3. If I do badly, I will fly below God's radar.

4. Either 1 or 2.

5. If I do well, I become vulnerable to tragedy—
   i.e., God's wrath.

   Therefore, I must incorporate
   the sufficient amount of suffering
   to obscure my wellness
   so that God does not smite
   what he either pities or cannot see.

   Or else God has mercy on those who find wellness—
   for how much suffering that involves.

   I can't say either way,
   but I know that sufferers' logic
   is the widest, straightest, flattest path to Hell.

5. God's escalator

If you stand on God's escalator,

you'll make it to the next floor
in the amount of time it would've taken you
to walk up regular stairs solely on your efforts—
and you'll block everyone behind you.

But if you walk up God's escalator,
you'll get there faster than both—
which, of course, doesn't matter to God.

6. Mobïan love

The further she departs from me,
the more closely she approaches me.

Only a sphericity of love
can divine *us* as what endured
and didn't need ideas.

7. Boredom

God never gets bored
because God knows He is never alone—
that He always spends time with himself.

'Existential states' are only for those
who have made the material *their ideal*.

8. Churched

My dad and his drinking friends
call going beyond the limit of drunkenness—
when drunkenness passes from itself to sleepiness—
"going to church" or "being churched."

They are ignorant Nietzscheans
who link church to being exhausted by folly,
to the time when the party is already over
but continues in the form of its slow decline.

I've read all the Nietzsche shit.
And as loathsome as Nietzsche found the Christians,
he never denied the possibility
that the creatures crawling out from the floorboards
we called "Christians"
really are beautified by the artificial light of Christ.

Nietzsche denied with good-will—
and he was a better *Christian* (which is a form)
for not believing in Christianity (which is a substance).

I've taken to going to church with my mother,
to observe her in her element.

I'm writing this on the back of a receipt.
The IRS might find this and put me on a watch-list.
It's probably illegal
to be unemployed for as long as I have
when you're as able-bodied as I am.

My mother hands me
some Church paper to write my sin on.
"Nah," I say, "I'll go to Hades for that.
I'll stick with the receipt.

The receipt's neutral—I can't defile it."

(Wow. Maybe X wanted someone neutral
to write her romance on—
because she can't ruin something neutral.
Of course, I am far from neutral,
and my ruin made me more spirited and attractive.
Papers crumbled up
and books vivisected with underlines
show more signs of life
when they are unfolded or read again.)

The elderly crawl into here with renewed life.
The arthritis sweats out.
Disney's dancing skeletons don't do these folks justice.
There is something dangerous about liver spots.
Life scars you no matter what.
Everyone is gifted by suffering.

I'm jealous of the elderly that outlasted sexuality.
I want their benefits.
They secretly don't need the pity everyone gives them.
They age like boxers—eyes swollen shut with glory.
They look cooler in sunglasses than you do.
I could cry at any moment.

The piano lady here is a dime—
and I can't even tell when she misinterprets the music.
The mistakes make me feel like I'm part of the process.

The old women here worship my mother.
They tell me how much they love her.
"Everyone does," I always say.

Old, southern women are as comforting as their food
and more fun than the *country-flavored* ones

closer to my age.
Their dumpy bodies that look like hand-made biscuits
don't bother them—
I bet they'll make you cum faster than Selena Gomez
because they never learned how.
They are all magic, no room for body.
Their beauty is not intuitive—
and says *"Bodies don't matter."*
My personality detracts from my looks.
But the wonderful old ladies never believe me
when I tell them.

Here, I'm the Gatsby
and the Emperor of Ice Cream
and Hemingway's title would've been cleverer
had it been about someone losing their arms.
I'm dreaming of anarchists and cheerleaders
power-clashing and consummating their love
with children.
The young women here are all gorgeous.
They all know something I don't—
and I never ask them what it is, because it's theirs.
They inherit the smiles of the babies
they talk to without 'baby voices'.
The babies constantly interrupt the sermon,
but not the spirit.

Of the chorus, I hear only one voice.
I'm being unfair in the wrong place.
But for now, I'll call her the cream of this crop—
and how some flowers
can beautify the muck
from which they stretch themselves,
yawn
and fall back asleep until next year.
The skeletons in this place all contribute

to single her out—
and I'm thankful they do.
(They should start serving mediocre meals
to make the desert tastier.)
She is totally unavailable.
She has a husband
who's average looking enough to appreciate her.
He's impregnated her
with what might be the next Christ.
And best of all,
her fiancée is too caught up in the Gospel
to catch me looking.

There is something to this Christ thing—
and it could make me Christian
if *the something whatsoever* never made itself clear.
I mean, shit,
I've felt more alive accepting the impossibility
of her ever becoming mine
(she'd still belong to Christ if she wasn't married)
than all my former pursuits combined.
I guess all this time I've been an Atheist to test God—
and He performed miracles
without coming off as eager to please.
I respect that.

There is more Otherness in this simplicity, this Xanadu,
than anywhere else on Earth—
I've never even been anywhere else,
this is how capitalism works everywhere—
the system is a spiritual machine (to quote old Ray).

9. Skepticism achieved

Bukowski could have met Burroughs but declined.
Van Zandt turned Dylan down on multiple occasions
when asked to collaborate.
Baudrillard said "God exists,
but I do not believe in Him,"
which is like being called to heaven by God
and turning him down.
Newcombe turned down a million-dollar deal
with Island Records
like Zuck turned down a million—
because the Napster mentality
is "fuck a million; a billion is cooler."

Hip hop and Townes and Zuck and Buk and Newc
have something in common.

This 'thing' they share
is not substantial, but formal.

They are seducers. Skeptics.
They are *good Americans*—
and thus *good globalists*
that have no ideology
(I can't say this about Zuck for sure—
the movie version of him might be cooler,
and how American *that* is).
Anti-capitalism is bourgeois!

America is skepticism achieved.
The television that distracts you
schools *me* in selective attention.
I can watch two TVs,
listen to music on my headphones,
and surf the web

as I read obtuse philosophical texts.
Shit, the multiplication of distractions
allows me to love children
(by mostly ignoring them).

Hyperreality is the concrete form of skepticism—
skepticism accidentally become praxis—
that occurs when reality renders itself suspicious
in the excess of its liberation.

We know nothing and are not lacking in reality.

The difference between poetry and narrative
is that poetry brings you into the process
from beginning to end.

"I'm going to show you how I'm gonna destroy
this fucked up system,"
said Anton at the beginning of *Dig*.

And guess what: *he wasn't lying*.

Of course,
the editors couldn't show the reality of his simulation.

10. The former lovers and me

Past lovers came out of the woodwork
to 'reconnect' with her.
They were like restaurant managers
who linger around your table to chat
and ruin your meal
that was going to be an escape from talking
in favor of chewing.

Her love life had serious indigestion problems—
and the coke he was giving her
was too pure to act as a laxative.

The only way for me to exist
in a state of exception within her contact list
was to leave her the fuck alone,
to fuck alone,
and rush out quickly enough
to forget some shit she will keep as mementos.

She is so afraid she needs tangible objects
to convince her our love existed—
but I keep nothing.

I don't need to.
I never questioned its reality or believed in it.

I am brave enough to internalize parts of the ones I loved
and still love—that 'reminders' become excessive.

So, I'm walking around sporting her mannerisms
and using her words:
"100%. Homie. Dope. Cute"
…I never said that common shit before.

But I guess I'm cooler now.

11. My weekly opiate

Almost each week I go to church.

I get to see beautiful women

whose Sunday's bests are made obsolete by their smiles.
I get to see what beauty looks like
when it begins and when it ages
and even when it never emerged
and left no harried traces in its disappearance.
Even the meth-head lady
who has the same figure when you look at her
from ahead/behind or from either side—flat…
even she is made wolf-like,
even she slows down for a moment.

I get to see people
who've known each other their whole lives
see one another each week
as if they were welcoming each other home from war.
Out in the world, this world,
I don't often get to see people
who are happy to see one another.

I get to see life-long musicians and singers
slide into home-base with their gifts, each ruled safe,
like Ray Charles' fingers across the piano.
A young woman from my graduating class
has the best voice I've ever heard,
and it will never leave her—
and it will never leave this nook
to be 'enjoyed' by the masses,
and it won't go to waste
for its strictly limited audience.

I get a free concert, free, no questions asked comradery
and free compliments
every single week
from this god-like soup kitchen of simplicity.

I am op'ed up on graciousness—

how could my chronically ill life
not have ended up here?

This Grace that could give itself to anyone—
even to everyone—
and yet concentrates itself and gives itself to me only,

and might even do this for all those who let it.

It's the artificiality of grace that makes it blessed.

I don't meet many people
who are thankful for my presence.

12. Hope

I hope that the evil I did
carries the magic of church and wine and the Holocaust
and turns from the worst thing to ever happen to you
to the best thing to ever happen to you—
just like the beneficence of the evil you did me.

Then, there would be two of us
dreaming of having changed the other's life
and being right—
but satisfied, like evil, in possibly not being right.

13. She shamed and blamed me

I don't blame her.
Men are shit so far as my experience goes,
and I have the man-parts,

so it's easy to mistake me for one of them.
I'd be an asshole too if I had to live in New Orleans—
that city that turns me off
like a woman too conscious of herself
who tries too hard to convince me she's sexy.
I'd be an even worse asshole
if I was studying to become a lawyer
and had to be around those fake-it-to-make-it pansies.

Nevertheless, I finally got out of her way
so she'd have no one to blame but herself.

Isn't that what most of them—the responsible ones—
want from us?

So, I disappeared—
and felt just short of, or bypassed altogether, resentment.

I didn't and still don't blame her.
I even blamed myself
without feeling ashamed for either being responsible
for 'too much'
or 'not enough'.

I don't enjoy the likely possibility
she may still be poisoning her own air
as I am freshening mine.
But I don't dwell on trivialities.

14. Two ambiguously related stanzas

To feel extraterrestrial warmth through glass
is still magical.
The technology does not give off that warmth

that isn't felt on the glass
but can be felt passing through it.
But technology warms me in the wintertime,
so I don't outright dismiss it.
What about X?
Is she the glass or the tech sort of medium?
Glass is more like a direct line to God;
but technology generates such a vastness
in what is little
that it may as well be God Himself.

My family still gathers,
but each time, *at the moment*, the members
find themselves looking forward or backward—
and each gathering ends up being a format.

Perhaps these two stanzas are related.
Perhaps not.
These things are complicated.

15. Googled myself

I Googled myself
and because nothing came up
I knew I was still in the process
of inventing myself
with names that don't exist yet
because of the way *I* use them,
except in the fact that I use them,
words there are not so many, too many,
search results for.

If you find yourself Googling me,
remember it's a previous me you'll find results for

and never me now—
since I don't even necessarily know that me,
always just getting acquainted with every single new me
before they leave without saying goodbye.

And I sure as shit
don't stall myself with the predictive text
of a search engine.

16. What I can never say to my father

One day there will be a person in my place
and a life in the place of my life
that will look nothing like this me in transition
and that older, stiffer me
from which I am in the process of departing.

One day my shore may be so distant
it will be invisible,
and you might be the only one
who claims to still see it
and that might make you appear crazy
to all my fellow travelers on the boat *that I am.*

One day you might be the only one
who has not gotten on *my* boat
and all the other fellows on it
may throw you overboard for complaining about me
while getting to experience the drunken ride.

You and me both must get out of my way
so that this course that isn't charted with *"of course"*
may make the shore disappear in favor of a new one
that grows visible from a distance that creates visibility.

But I also might be so kind as to let you ride with me
as you complain the whole way—
and I will give you *your* charm,
I will call it your own, unoriginal curmudgeonliness.
And even the most unoriginal things
like soap
can become artful in their meta-mentality—
and how silly that is!

Anyway, it may still be the case
that the "me" you've been talking shit about
for a while now never even existed
anywhere except in your head.

And you should pride yourself on your creativity.

17. No ruler of the game, just the game itself—that's
    greater than the sum of the players

The game itself is unhackable
but fits to you when you fit to it,
that is, can be 'partnered with'.

And the good sportsmen
all treat the game as another player
who is better than they are,
always simultaneously winning with each winning team
and losing with each losing team.

No one is hipper than God
(God is the ground of Being and the Game itself,
who no player is bigger than).

Bataille tried to cheat the game
and play with religion without being seduced by God.

Ironically or post-ironically
or whatever you want to call it—
since God is a "substance" that can "create anything
and be created out of anything"—
when I learn to be happy with anything at all
that's when I will receive the gift
I am destined for and that is destined for me.

Good fortune lets itself be seduced
even by those who speak against it—
and always comes out learning something
and curious to learn others
the hard way.

18. Your friendly neighborhood creep

I know that I have always been present
and haven't truly changed
only because your love was greater
than it should've been at your age
and attached itself to my potential
and never to my powers,
which exist only at one place
at one time.

You weren't the first to 'really' know me,
and you weren't the last—
and that's partly because of how I present myself
to the ones *I can love*
because they are kind enough to let me.

You saw where I was going before I did,
though,
and between the two of us, you saw me first.

19. Love appreciation

I never thought it'd happen once
and when I thought it had happened again
for the first and final time,
I still wondered why it was so good
and yet much worse than I could've ever imagined.

And yet it happened twice in a row,
and the second one was a much sweeter deal
and the first injury had already healed,
like a soft mood whose transitions are not assertions,
and I was ready for the first time the second time—
like Jesus when he returned as proof of Himself,
having united with Himself only after death.

The first one I wanted to love me
when I was at my worst.
But when I was at my worst,
she didn't merely not love me,
she seemed also to hate me for sharing my suffering—
the most precious binder
that is tinier and more numerous and more gelatinous
than chia seeds—
with her without warning.

I know for a fact that the second—
seeing as she was there when I was still being made—
would appreciate my vulnerability
and the gift of my worst.

And yet, for this second person,
I can never lead with suffering
since she has only been around when I was at my best,
during periods of physical or spiritual growth.
And during growth spurts, it only hurts at first
but eventually seems to have the potential
for happening automatically
in the background.

I even get the joy of *seeing* her for the first time,
when before it was only the good fortune
of good senses other than sight
that held onto her long enough
to have the opportunity of making an impression.

And I have always made impressions
everywhere I go
almost like my ancestors did virtuous deeds
to make life this easy for me.

The second one might get me—
if she happens to want to—
at this new point
where I not only make chance impressions
but have *learned* it, too, *as an art.*

My joy rushes things,
and I fell in love with myself too quickly
and with too much excitement to judge.

The first one loved the opposite way.

The second, I think, is capable of both,
so that her appreciation of *my* way
would constitute a decision and not a prejudice.
The first got in the way of the love I gave her

from start to finish.

The second, I think, might be out of the way,
but not so out of the way
I'm no longer willing to go the extra mile
beyond the extra mile *I already give*
to everyone I meet but never marry.

And I think the second could be sturdier
and not crumble under the pressure of my devotion,
which would be great if she looks for excuses.

20. A fork that closes again and so cannot be used as a utensil to deliver nourishment

Utensils are mine, used by my hands only
and washed accordingly afterwards.

But I see this fork going two ways
to one place:

Either you're prepared for my love or not.
If you're not, you may be eventually
or you may never be.
If you're not, but may be eventually, then you will be
eventually,
and we will already be best friends at that point.
If you're not and may never be, then you will never be,
and we will still be best friends.

So, either you love me or you're my best friend
or both—
but if you stop loving me, you stop being my best friend,
and isn't that something?

21. Morality is not for everyone, but it works for some who
    were built for it historically

    Once you've learned the extent to which
    your mood affects other people,
    how could you not appreciate the love
    of those who let you get away
    with the poisons they willingly drink from your pores,
    even with the glaring skull and cross bones on the label?

    But then again,
    isn't it the folks who understand their suffering
    and appreciate love accordingly—

    isn't it *they* who are fit for love,
    to both give it and receive it
    or even take it away.

    And isn't it they too
    who really bring suffering *to the table?*

22. Revived [relived (relieved)] chance

    She showed up again
    and with such vogue and such little-ness
    that she brought Chance itself 'with' her,
    not only individual chances.

    But it wasn't the old, monstrous clump of clay
    Chance once was—that Yahweh of certain doom.
    It was a chiseled, rounded, smaller,
    softer, squishier,
    more cuddlable and clutchable Chance—
    a newborn baby Chance,

more the God disintegrated by prophecy,
a chance readability
that repeats itself to always surprise you
in surprising new forms
you didn't expect "surprise" to take.

She showed up again with her *usual* gifts of possibilities,
which never wear out,
but not because they never actually form.

She has given me more with her small appearances—
that seem to never end,
that seem to give memory an *artful* purpose
other than the past's *survival*—
than anything money will ever buy me.
She is homelier than a house.

Her love, whether she means it or not,
says "No longer must you have to use your powers
for evil."

Her love makes me think the unthinkable,
like Chance that is not human
and yet risks itself *for me*.

Her love contradicts itself without apology
as it holds itself in suspension and in potential.
I'm living off it now
and she has no idea I am and will continue to
even if she never finds out—
not that I wouldn't love to share my love for her
with her
and not keep it to myself for just myself alone.

Her love makes it clear my apologies are unnecessary,
that we are always-already good.

Her love keeps coming back,
always new, like jazz,
and each time it does—
I might be a little more deserving of it.

Her love is inviting
without being spoken or written or sent—
and never sexual,
but always erotic.
It goes without saying—
"I'm not going to tell you what I think.
But anything is possible.
I *could* be thinking anything, even about you"
is something that might've *occurred to you,*
which is now *occurring to me*—
so that, if it occurred at all,
it had to occur to both of us.

Chance lets itself be known or *experienced*
by chance—prodigality.
But it will eventually happen
within a not-narrow spectrum
of constitutions that are potencies—
because it too is potent,
potent enough to die by climax.

Her love never had to be convincing.
It was poetic—not literary!

Her love says
"Ariel, you were *always* a poet.
You're so creative
you don't need shit to write.
Make a move."

Her love could have been stronger,
but obscured itself
and weakened itself enough
to give me something to add,
something to do,
something to achieve.

Her love let me have the glory of work—
a sort of volunteer work that isn't just charity—
that brings me into a process *from the beginning*
even when her mind was already *made up*,
neatly, like a bed,
so that I couldn't win her if I tried.

Her love could have taught me
that when the world gets better, I get better
and when I get better, so does the world,
but also that we might all get worse together.

Her love was complete,
American
and yet never got boring as it never changed.

Her love—
even when it ignored me, it did so with grace.

Together,
we would plausibly never get hung up on one another
and there would still plausibly be no hang-ups
to our relationship that drags nothing behind it.

23. Tranquility

Things almost always work out

better than I meant them to—

and I don't even low ball myself with expectations,
like those people who always have to win
against their shit judgments about themselves
to be happy about results.

I don't know why this is.

I'm eerily similar to Donald Trump—
"Don't blame me, blame the voters;
I never asked for this success,
they just gave it to me.
I don't know. I don't read into it.
That's your job, newsman.
Why don't you tell me who's to blame?
If you say me, I'll go with that.
I don't argue; that's your job."

But without precedence, and unlike the President,
I'm not conceptual, so I don't require confirmation.

24. Gravity reunited

What is up must go down,
so throw so high that what is thrown,
even though it falls faster from a greater height,
takes longer to make it back to you.

Maybe even throw so hard
that it goes higher than gravity and enters orbit—
i.e., when it's still tied down to gravity
but not heavy enough to reach earth
until long after your death.

If it's light enough to make it up there,
it's light enough to come back down eventually.

25. When did the artists get so hip?

The artists are super hip.
Their lives seem like parties.
Wtf is pathos to these cool as shit artists?
They all have that beauty
that only good healthcare
diet
bed
vitamins can bring.
We all grew up watching marathons
while we were sick,
wtf could we have to say?
Shit, I was even ashamed to write
looking as good as I do,
being as affluent as I am,
but they are even better looking than me,
wtf could they have to say?
Some of the punks in here still
know how to fuck up and look like shit—
which isn't even invisible!
They sport unfunctional styles and demeanors
and haircuts.
At least they are sitting down here with me
as everyone else slow dances
to all the cool, *happening* art sacking the pathos
out of this superstructural cheese party.

When art is good, its unacceptable.
But that doesn't mean what is unacceptable

is good art.

26. The salutary flag

Sometimes I roll my eyes
like moderate slot machines with no guts to spill
at all this freedom going to waste,
all this space left for crime that belongs to people,
that is being reserved
for the white collar, not-gonna-get-fucked-in-the-ass
criminals.

I want to live in the deserted spaces
where I can't get caught doing *anything*,
even though there's nothing to do but crime.
I'm not brown enough for it to matter.

The rappers are rapping
their anarchist philosophy of peace,
but you just listening to the hook.

"All this mainstream freedom ain't shit."

The criminals are alts.
Nothing's hipper than crime.
Jesus's homies were freedom-desiring criminals,
some criminal simply in the fact that they exist—
fucking ugly stupid poor assholes.

And the homies prolly know better than any
how red the neck of the freedom—
that government cheese—
really is.

27. Untitled haiku series 5

We have in common
similarly rupturing
experiences.

Something so perfect
that it repeats forever
cannot be trusted.

You cut out errors
like tumors of teeth and hair,
are vague about it.

Won't go word for word
like I'm matching on a blunt,
which is prudential.

Micropoetry:
leave it to the computer
with no history.

28. Entertainment Tonight and Death

Michael Strahan [autocorrected by Microsoft,
which doesn't understand apophenia]
to permanently join Good Morning America.
~~I'm free to kill myself.~~
Gwen Stefani only gets to keep 2 of her 5 homes
after the divorce.
~~I'm free to kill myself.~~
Jennifer Aniston once teased for her bubble butt
named top 50 most beautiful people
by Entertainment Magazine.

~~I'm free to kill myself.~~
Dance Moms daughter worth $2 million at 13.
~~I'm free to kill myself.~~
Kate Hudson and James Franco have great birthdays.
~~I'm free to kill myself.~~
Co-stars have feuds behind the scenes.
~~I'm free to kill myself.~~

29. it all

The beauties are stupid
and the intellectuals are ugly
and the smart and sexy suck at fucking
and the fatties fuck the best, but are too nice,
and the bitches make better companions, but cheat,
and the faithful are needy and incomplete
and the good looking don't feel good
and the best skin for aging is covered with pimples
and the clear skin gets wrinkles too quickly
and the big tits sag
and the perky tits stay put, but cannot be fucked,
and the people with things figured out
are just ahead of themselves,
and tbh, never catch up with themselves,
but damn up their future
and call the accumulation of drift "ME."

If I were an honest, devotional lover with a list,
I'd have made it by now.

But I treat my craft no different than potential mates—
can't even commit to my greatest gift.

Only waste feels free…

because no one wants to use it.

Don't let those love hippies recycle you.

30. Not another fucking surrealist trashcan

The page is a trashcan of shit words
that I could have recycled but threw away instead
like a small-time terrorist
shoveling in his small portion to the shit heap.

The world is 'fucking' the earth
or the earth is going and fucking itself through us,
and still the responsibility falls on me to fucking save it?

Language is a shifty prostitute, easily advertised,
and it is 'fucking' speech
or fucking itself through ads
and still the responsibility falls on me
to say 'something'?

Fuck nah.
The page is the grating in the sewer drain
accumulating airplane bottles,
funded by people that hate money enough
to break the bank
on someone who's not faking crazy—
bottles licked clean by tongues left homeless
by a lack of sharp teeth,
that first alphabet.

Y'all some dumpster-diving motherfuckers
reaching into my past as deep as the toilet bowl,
never there in the first place.

My head's in this virtual oven
as I watch with the fascination of the atom bomb
at my leftovers sucked warm by the microwave.

So maybe the poem doesn't become trash
until it enters consciousness,
becomes God, not-me,
or maybe it only gets G'd up, becomes not-me
because I offered it up for someone else
sweet enough to take it off my hands
and make it therefore unattractively acceptable.

I will hate myself through you, lover.

31. Handmade

Whatever can be made solely by means
of machines without operators
will have less demand
than whatever is produced solely
by the hands of human beings.

Labor is a cool medium
between the demands for inexpensive products
and products made too cheaply and automatically.

Labor is a demand,
an object of consumption,
and consumers will obsess over sourcing their products
to peasants liberated and alienated by the work provided
by demand itself,
and without a doubt, consumers pride themselves
on the jobs their consumption provides.

They don't want a product made automatically.
They want a product that is invested time
that could've been spent doing anything else.

They'll castrate you to make it easier to rest on you
as you bend over backwards,
then complain when you're not in the mood.

32. Cpt

Don't let them get you in a hurry
and change the way you relate to time,
even if they've programed your circadian rhythms.

When I didn't have a job, I never looked at the time,
but now I want to know how soon 'til I get off,
how much time has disappeared
and how much left
of this nasty short end of the cigarette's pace
I have to burn and waste on productivity.

I'm not going to let them
have me counting down the hours
or the calories
or the days in a year.

They do the scheduling for me.
They're job is to manage me...
I'm not going to manage me.

I glide over my wishy-washy schedule like a pelican
and return from each dive with a heavy mug
full of repressed death wishes,

'til I empty myself mid-flight.

33. Curiosity

At work, they ask one another
what's going on
and they always respond "Nothin man. Workin."

The concrete and the abstract made equivalent
by this tangible estrangement.

34. Online origins (online base)

Me: If I were interesting, you'd want to meet me, right?

Them: I think I'd like to get to know you first.

Do they read the script before they see the film?

I bet they don't.

But they want to turn meeting into crystallized labor
by producing from accumulated knowledge
applied knowledge that ends in its objectification,
in 'closeness',
where physical proximity
is the dead labor of a prescriptive exchange
that signifies *communication itself,*
where communication
is the purported use value of language,
but always ends up being its exchange value.

I cannot be understood, except through senses.

And the bit gathering and bit producing intellect
is very concretely not included in the five.

35. The hyper-Law that has absorbed anarchy

If I had no gag reflex,
I'd shut up, let the Law take my breath away
and trust me not to use teeth.

If they entered me deep enough,
it wouldn't even be considered swallowing my pride.

See how mysteriously bodily functions metamorphose
when their everyday intersectionality
is transubstantiated into flow charts
by penalization.

36. new alterations

Every time I meet a new woman, I think

"Goddamnit, I'm going to have to change my strategy
and discover the angles
that make someone new cum."

Then I think "Is porn fake sex
or is sex fake porn?"

I almost always consider sex interactive porn

like how kindness is just interactive morality
and how morality is just interactive God
or whatever.

37. Work

The whites secretly hate it
and resist it with accomplishment and skill
head on.
The blacks stay cool, secretly deriding it,
and move with hot rhythm—
dancing around it the more intense it gets,
giving the snide appearance that they enjoy it,
debasing anyone who believes them
because who could be stupid enough
to believe people enjoy their alienation
besides white people.

The Asians neither hit the task head on,
hating it in secret,
nor give the appearance of enjoyment
or technicity of movement.
They just do it…like the best Criminals.

Me? I copy bits of each
and oscillate between those settings:

I hate it,
dance around it,
and let it run its course through me
like the fabled butcher's knife
that never touches the beef because it's so sharp.

38. like it's illegal

She gave a look of imminent death
of a lack of oppression, choice or compatibility,
without vital phantasmagoria
like we were plotting the revolution and were aware
of all the blood without delineable origins
that would make us sport the same colors.

Kim K's book of selfies will have captured
all the faces our luck might interpret as hostile.

And yet we will not act
nor name an enemy so simply
for whom disappearance is possible,
to realize the illusory dialectic
as if relativity were as simple as 1 2.

We will instead
keep the superfluity in its boorish intensity
to this unformed secret society,
not comparable to primitives or the State.

I will do everything worthwhile
with a secret
like it's illegal.

39. Warm yellow lights

The dehydrated piss, crystalline yellow eminence
of caution lights
waves the externalized tremolo
of the reel to real longline
from foot to head,

40. For 'writers'

Don't do it when it's necessary
or when there's a demand for it
or when it sells
or when it's reproducible
or when it saves
or when it garners immediate attention or goes viral
or when it inspires.

Don't do it when the content is a memory
or a dream.
Don't do it when it seems 'right'
or historical
or natural
or original
or copy.

Don't do it unless your insides
are dying a slow agonizing death,
but not from starvation.
You need your energy.

Don't do it unless the disease
or the stress
or the symptom
is of ambiguous origin or all in the head.

Don't do it when you know
the good wine valleys or years,
when your dick isn't thinking for you
because you're surfeited,
when your managing your money
and thinking economically.

Don't do it unless it is conscious of its own silence,

of the potential for another Dark Age.

Just don't do it for anything or anyone,
not even for yourself,
because you must suspect even yourself
of false consciousness.
THEY're doing it
AGAIN

and

AGAIN

'creating' [modifying] poems like 'characters' [avatars]
every time a NEW GAME is started.

Don't do it if it's for ambiance
or atmosphere
or effect
or consequence
or itself.

Don't do it if it kills Whitey, but not capitalism.

Don't do it if it kills truth but not mystery
and doesn't extend uncertainty.

Don't do it if it gets you endorsements
or into a mag
or wins the contest
when it's success is a function
of the finesse with which it jerks its readers
or a party
society
species
organ.

That's be too easy.

But you can't *value* skepticism either.

41. A close second

Tanning in the sun,
a walrus on a rock,
sweating like a shroom shading ants
or a tall black man wearing loose-fitting activewear
is a close second to death.

A trance-like depression
that won't speak the name of the thing
person
Idea
that won't go quietly from the head
is a close second to death.

And you can't lose to death
and expect them to call your name.

The honorable mentions
are like sequins to snakeskin.

42. Nothing, after nihilism stops using it, becomes interesting

Any porn will do.
Any job will do.
Any parents would have done.

Any point in time would have done,
but they didn't—HERE I AM.

Any president will do.
Any conversation topic will usually do.
Any nation would have done.
Any appearance, style, explanation would have done,
but they didn't,
and I'm not grateful to luck.
The State or my family or employer didn't invent that.
If *anything*, God, but who knows?

Things are what they are. Anyone can say that.
It means what it means.
Anyone could have been anyone
saying that about anything.

If things are good now, they might be better later.
There is no best time ever
best poem ever
best relationship ever of life
and if there is, you're lazy
tired
or intellectually unconscientious
or trapped
with nothing to entertain but mental cardio
mental card tricks
or mental cable.

But I don't care you ended up being what you are.
Just telling *it like it is*.
I'm not against lazy,
just against bad reasoning
and theories of legitimacy,
of what is or isn't alienating.

43. The exceptional

If "there is an exception to every rule,"
there must be an exception to the rule
that there are exceptions to every rule
and perhaps a rule to which there are no exceptions.

Tell me something I cannot deny
or leave me be
and don't rule out the possibility
that you nourish your law with anarchy
like suction-cup therapy
that will cause open sores
if placed in the same area too often
in too short a time.

44. Similitude & Tinder

I see their faces one after the other
like a flip book in which nothing elapses,
and there is only one emotion, I wonder which?

I see their distance by the mile in the vicinity
and they are
5
8
29 miles away
and they all are the same as me
as each other
and they all might as well be lightyears away or not even
exist—
I'll never meet any of them
and they'll never meet me

because there is no half-way.
I don't fault them,
it's probably impossibly to choose one from a million,
divided more easily by the profusion of options
and managed in our acute, chronic indecision,
especially when only one sense—
and perhaps the weakest, the visual sense—
is activated only once the code is inputted and scanned.

45. The kitchen

The barrier between kitchen and dining room
gives the food the mystical quality only matched in price
of having appeared by the diner's wishes alone.

The satisfaction of 'consumer needs'
makes time seem like it has never existed until now
in an automated, auto-updated world—
a present necessary and total yet already made irrelevant
by the data documented to make you a demographic,
real-time having always already passed a second ago.

46. Thick girls

The squishy women never wear belts
and are always wriggling up their weeping trousers,
maybe even curling their toes
like rockets exploding right off the platform
or just explosions on TV in general.

Or at least I watch both with the same secret wishes,
hidden joys

and outer politeness.

The more I think about it,
the more inefficient the state apparatus seems
for letting me live,
considering it could get 'my' money—
'its' money—
from somewhere, anywhere else.

47. Two exercises

The infantile pleasure
of the exertion of one's own motors,
unconscious of one's potential
and thus shocked at one's own powers,
the ecstasy of power
achieved by the abstraction of bodies
in their becoming-speech
through the condensed, automated habits
the reps
refined and become need across generations of servitude

or a play-acting in the safe-zone of the created,
intended, unlike blind necessity, to transfer knowledge,
for initiates are only alien in their becoming,
not in their essence.

48. #fetish poems big in Q3 2017

Online, you could tell me every last detail
of every last orifice and every last surface
and all there is to know about what you'd do to me

let me do to you,
and to your friends,
until the boredom is a boner kill

But I'd still want to fuck you
because I haven't heard your voice yet.

No *amount* of information can break that pact.

49. Amateurs

Watching people fuck
is like watching people
desperately seeking something they were told is possible
and falling desperately short,
but denying the shortcoming
with the rehearsed enthusiasm you spit to the boss.

They are fucking super hard
fast
deep
going limp as the blood lost returns to the brain
that isn't buying
and the women seem to get less and make more noise,
however the two are related.

They are fucking like recently freed slaves
entering incarcerative social processes
they developed no defenses to on the plantation.

They are fucking
like they believe good sex is out there somewhere
or that *sex is what you make it*,
then they smack the ass

to get their head back into the game
after they've noticeably lost interest several times over.

Porn and the madness of a Saturday night
in the claustrophobia of statistically accurate enjoyment
that has the visible certainty of a man's cum—
both exhibit the lucidity
of their own illusoriness and impossibility.

The amateurs chase the magic dragon
right out of my way,
for never wanting their sloppy seconds.

50. Dalmatian

Your spots are becoming patches
from all the stress of being pulled in different directions
on that torture rack of the mixed messages
of a hodgepodge culture
that makes little sense in the early twenties
without the help of straw dog representations
whose convenience will make things worse if rebelled.

And those about to dash into flaming corridors
with collapsing ceilings and floors
in outfits that ruin agility
need spotted friends.

51. Not much to say

I don't have much to say about you.
Everything seems in order.

Everything seems to be functioning.
Everything seems there
like a forest I don't have much to say about
because I know that even if my presence alters it,
it functions without me.

I don't have much to say about you.
It's probably a good thing I don't—
it could mean that your presence isn't functioning for me
like a mystification or an alienation, an illusion.
I can feel it and I can feel you feeling it
and I can feel you feeling me feel it—
the amps pointed at the amps
and that could mean
we won't ever need to finish each other's sentences
because the mind will dissolve behind the eyes,
but you will interrupt it by asking me
in a voice better than the digital remaster, "What?"
Because then when I answer "Nothing,"
my mind will race to the explanation
until it becomes a self-conscious asymptote.

Words repeat, we both know it,
we're older and we've heard them,
probably all of them before,
but I'm embarrassed the drink—
like the religious narcotic
or the philosophy narcotic
or the art narcotic—
conjured up all those words
because I could've just stared at you all night.
I'd never go cross-eyed.
I'd be as lucid as ever,
and you'd completely understand everything.

Even if I only saw you that one time that one night,

you'd become an effect of me
and I'd become an effect of you
factually and scientifically,
and you'd be part of this chain that's been driving me
to only want my words
to hit reality in the most understandable way possible
without becoming mirrors
of the abstractions of estranged labor,
retaining their little meanings
and only changing their difference
according to their historical nature.

I'm not upset Lou Reed already made pale blue eyes
into a commodity—
yours have seen me,
and I promise I won't make them signify for me.

How could an alien like me be so downed to earth?

52. Don't let luck confuse you

Sometimes it's the other getting lucky with you.

53. on cocaine

I'm holding on
but only like I hold my bladder—
I'm ruining it with patience and fortitude
for the sake of business.
I'm not going anywhere
but I AM doing multiple things at once.

The music is sounding better temporarily

the colonization of the wetlands/
Disneyworld is starting to look like a needle aimed at mars
and THE KIDS WILL FINALLY STOP NAGGING
AND SHUT THE FUCK UP
so you can get the high score
or see the preview for next week's episode
the women are appearing beautiful
unique
like they'll reject me, but they won't
like they'll stay fashionable, fit and 17 forever
and they will, whether I or they like it or not.

The trees are almost interesting
as if geology, biology and ecology
aren't complete sciences.
I'm no longer rooting
for the storms, the floods, the fires
to swallow the golf courses like goose-feathers.
I'm doing the chores
with a pep in my step.
Happiness is an easy sell:
people look for immediate gain,
you sell them tangible, tactile profit
and fuck them in the long run
just as easily as you sell them the slow accumulation
and fuck them day to day.
I'm trusting happiness.
It's damn near ideological
I'm as simple as a Yuppie.
I'm jumping from invention to invention like a Millennial
pretending that the 80s & 90s never happened.
I'm not a rerun or a reaction
or a fly living long enough to eat, fuck and die.
THOUGHT IS NO LONGER TEMPORARY
the drugs are standing in for the computer
my parents
media, everything.
I'm not upset my mother said once she's in heaven—

the big incubator filled with heroin and Muppet Babies
in the sky—
she'll never know I even exist.
And finally, the programming
the HOW-TO videos
the women, the condos, Chelsea boots & iTunes playlists—
all the possibilities and easiest solutions
are starting to reflect my desire.

The cocaine is strong
but something up there is more realistic
than the reward center
and even the cocaine cannot make me forget
that the only resolution we have
is the sliding scale of the television menu.
I'm high but I'm not part of the culture
and I wouldn't advocate it or miss it
when the dealers have gone straight.

54. Activation

We're *highly* inactive,
but activated by the Code.

55. the bad, or the critique of *good fortune*

Subtract all the bad
and the good doesn't come naturally

but the lack of the good isn't bad *in itself.*

56. A little unpretentious truth

It's no mystery why I like you.
Nothing grandiose about it—
as little mystery as the tiny follies
and utterly trivial activities
we bring to life with our humanity,
that feeds back between our eye contact in our stories
but never fully achieves itself,
only grows and grows without getting bigger,
with a self-awareness of this fact.

It's no mystery why I'm attracted to you.
Your body
your mind
are the fruits of social labor,
built upon cyclic experience,
critiqued by trial and error,
picked at the right time.
The generations
whole societies
and individuals and the animals they ate
have prepared you
(not for me, for existence)
the parents
teachers
physicians
designers
textile workers
beauticians
plumbers
crane operators
meat processors
field hands
the mechanics
janitors

philosophers
bus drivers and bus boys
have all made you beautiful.

And even the pedestrians, by occupying spaces,
have made a way for you to slip in here
for me to glimpse and consider unnoticed
and all the things that have eaten you
beaten you
or loved you
have bottlenecked you here before me.
There's almost no one I wouldn't thank.

You're one of the best parts of humanity—
it's base—
the part that's everywhere,
even in the cut paths
the underbrush sometimes hasn't yet reclaimed,
the part that turns nature to world—the labor.

It's an exception to look at the product
and appreciate all the life put into its own existence.

We only appreciate the function
relative to the consumer.

57. Nothing says I love you

Work is the escape and the prison,
but the human relations can vanish
while the body at least has the symbolic decency
to decay.

Right away, I decided *already*

you were going to leave—
it's your way
and being left is my way.
But I hope you consider
that my hesitation to *change my life*
doesn't make me a nihilist prude—
things are different now:
I'm always at work,
I study life—
an average manifestation of it—
I'm doing research for a project
that will be explained better
by a future me looking back
when I have more to go on,
but look, I'm in the field, ok?

The flow of life hasn't,
might not take me to Tokyo or Beirut,
but there are jetliners and I'm too lazy to plan,
too cheap to have an agent
and too proud to be my own.
The money is the only thing
I'd be happy to get rid of.
My life or life itself
has had its rushes
with the widening and narrowing of the channel,
but the lazy river I'm taking hasn't shored me up
yet.

You were searching for the Other,
running from the Same—
travel, your escape and your prison—
but you're going to vanish from me, I know it.
I won't stop you,
while my intelligence has the symbolic efficacy
to contemporaneously let you go and cherish you.

I wanted to yell at you
to shake you
(or else just grabbing you sounds appealing now)
and tell you about the simple
the basic
the mean
the everyday
and the odyssey and road film that the day to day is
tell you that we travel through time unto death
at the speed of perception
and I don't want you impatient—
but you know these things,
I know you know,
and I'm not stupid, so you have to.

One day the life dims
and the gonads wag
and mind starts to look the wrong way,
where it's already been.
I don't want you to skip ahead.
I don't want you to base your consciousness
on the first half of your life,
but yes, everything in stages.
There's a time to win freedom *significantly*
(to signify freedom with wildness),
when freedom seems so strange,
so prudish,
that it seems likely only a beast could overtake it,
and there's a time to collect
and burden oneself with the absurd weight of moments,
the only value of which appears to be their quantity: one.
How else will you learn the value
of putting down all those moments
with the good intellectual conscience
that their collection was also a need?

I wanted to handcuff you to my arm,
but we'd go nowhere,
pulling each other in place, into stasis
trying to go our separate ways.
I just want you to pay more attention to the bare,
look at the desert
without the eye habitually moving to the pristine oases
the lush savannahs,
pay more attention
to your placement *in* the surrounding order,
to your own desertion—
desertification that coincides with your growth—
and how you want others
to habitually notice your lushness,
your pristine,
forgetting that you're more, way more,
this immense
immersive
prickly desert
equally capable of wisdom (the extension of the human)
and privation.

Pay more attention to the exchange
that simply being *already is*,
but I don't want you to think automatically
that you have to *do* anything differently.
If you already are great,
some extra effort can't hurt.
You can live freely,
but freedom is a process,
a good mental habit.
I want you free—but it takes work
I see you working hard.

I wanted you to see me as exotic,

as a wonder of the world
right here in a nameless, faceless suburb
at apparent random
whose photographic arts
really show they could've been taken anywhere.
I wanted to be an experience of the possible
in the (only apparent) contradiction.

If I recall,
the aliens crash landed in the nowhere zone.
I'm here living an average life,
writing poems that desire to be self-conscious,
in the activity on which they are based,
of the problematic obscurity,
and yet the equally problematic acceptability, in poetry.
I'm here leading a 'human' life
from some perspectives, but not all—
a productive life so far as the author is concerned
that desires to convalesce the perfunctory fantasy
in reality as perfect as an object given fixed value,
a common anomaly blending into the ambience of tones
that never overcome
or become distinct from one another.

I wanted you to have the guts of an acute hopelessness
so consistent it has no tears to underpin its honesty,
to have the everyday courage of everyday people
without potential for promotion,
to be ok, as ok as I am,
with the here and now, including *this* vacuous job
this vacuous area
this vacuous country
this vacuous time,
even when I'm despairing
over the impossibility of SOMETHING ELSE.

Don't worry,
I'm not going to love you
to your face or behind your back
if you don't want me to,
but you deserve it.
You're a good specimen
and I love humanity when it acts
almost like it thinks of itself in relation to itself
as other among others.
So, I will secretly love you in the form of a pact
since promises are broken
or become obliging bargains every day,
and yet here and now,
according to this society,
it seems nothing says "I love you"
more than isolating and ejecting oneself from the real—
the magic that exists
without proof
explanation
measurement
or monetary value,
the magic that never makes it to the Christmas card.

58. The Party

They're going to give you shit for it no matter what.
The petty shit they give you cannot do shit.
Their shit cannot act itself out,
cannot have a definition that isn't infinite,
cannot be itself,
and if it isn't even being shit, itself, then what can it
accomplish (without an accomplice—another entity)?

The shit that they give you

isn't different than Kool Aid or Goodyear tires
sharing ingredients
like reptiles and people share a common ancestor.
It won't make your dick look any different.
It won't give your BMs regularity.
The shit they 'give' (mandatorily!)
can't add up to a revolution.
It doesn't even seem to add up to a 'democratic' election
just CRISIS after CRISIS.

They're going to give you shit for it *no matter* what.
Let them take responsibility for the world.
Let them walk the treadmill and die
before never running out of episodes to stream.

They're going to give you shit for it *no matter* what.
Let them compare your shit poetry
to some successful poet
because they don't know shit
give a shit about shit
and yet the shit they *have* keeps piling up.

They're going to give you shit for it.
A tattoo is as ineffectual with regards activity
as the human body stamping itself
with all the jabberwocky of A and not A
like a peaceful coexistence of idiotic organs
that can't do shit
while the brain generates CONTENT after CONTENT.

All the shit is piling up.
The shit is piling up out of everyone's pockets
like coins weighing down the pockets
of scurvy-brained pirates
probably as keen on imaginary pussy
as on the heroin chic of any purchasable object.

They'll shit from any possible perspective
no matter how unrealistic
no matter how ineffectual
no matter how redundant.
They'll shit on you for your best
your worst
your stability
your inconsistency
and if you make a sound in their direction,
they'll come shit all the shit that's been shat on them
right down your ears that work as well as the eyes,
direct lines to the brain,
but the body doesn't do shit—
it just stands there communicating
doing nothing…just like the shit that they give.

59. 6669

The warm spot that she made
in my heart with her love:
that pee cloud. Swim around.

60. I'm going to burn this tattoo off

I'm going to do it like the meth head bikers:
with a metal coat hanger under flame,
in one swipe.
And you're going to help me
by not looking or holding my hand,
as if I never needed you there.

You're going to help me get this X off my pelvis
by ignoring me
and not letting me make you a vessel:

no more X's,
no more Muses or inspiration,
no more Other, Beyond, Sacred, Sublime
no more abjection, death obsession,
isolation mumbo jumbo,
no more of the unchecked habitual,
nothing new, but something deeper
slower
explicit
temporal.

You know, doing simple things with you
like helping you get out of work on time
brings a relation that is maybe not permanent,
but pertinent,
here and now even if it isn't top priority,
even if the future keeps death a secret.

I still want something real,
subject to death, the possibility of the impossible,
to false consciousness that always looms—
but something quiet
timely
with enough potential to not happen lazily all at once,
aware of the life left in it
that cannot go on the same way at each of its twilights.

61. not knowing the audience

Cocaine and shopping feel the same
the work mind is thicker than consciousness.
A dead body wouldn't get a response from me
when I'm on the clock.
A concussion would make me feel guilty
but I would move no more automatically than usual.

I'm becoming what I am
what I do
the shit mind
the concussed mind silent about its own agony
its slick deposal
a mind that isn't itself but can't tell
and never will
but can't accept that
do anything about it
or take responsibility.

I'm becoming like them
around them all the time.
I've become their microphone they keep checking
but is never on
until the feedback shrieks of self-perpetuating affects
and a petty relation.

I'm choking on the pettiness
attracting people who are dead
but pretend to be sad to entertain themselves
or the idea that little squabbles
add up to a coherent narrative,
not just a series of images.

I'm tuning them out
but myself out with them
because the stupidity of the expectations
the "discussions"

and the value summits
has dulled my radar
that no longer detects the direction of the objects
its silent noises recoil from.

The compensation is a joke
an insult
the customers aren't masters but that's worse
you're supplying the dick
and the asshole
the mouth and the cum
but you never get to see the tape.

I'm pissed
(like money but not away)
the drugs are slowly wearing off
the pussy is slowly wearing off
the philosophy is a drag
the world is unrelatable
the television is as petty as the workers
forgetting about their stupefaction via more stupidity
and me doing the same
but never being satisfied
falling for it
falling in love with another person
via my own detachment to falling for an ideal
a possibility
or a cause.

I'm a reaction
a woman
a primitive in the work camps
watching mothers and friends turning tricks
watching hyperviolent horror films
and seeing everyday life reflected sincerely,
as worried about my incapacity for suicide
as about my loss of self
of talent

of critical thought
but not worried about my future
because I'm certain there isn't one that I'd want.

The vagaries of resistance
that tantalize by staying on the tip of the tongue
like the margarita salt around the glass
really make you thirsty
but the alcohol is greater than you
like the system that no one can seem to grasp
but everyone knows they are getting fucked by.

62. Jailbait

The 60s were garish
with all that footage of stoner nudity
and immasculating conceptions
with that concrete sensuality—
the screen—
translates into *an effect of itself.*

They kicked Polanski out of the country.

I'm not sure about Woody Allen.

The 'roids in the meat
are hitting the women harder.
Then the birth control makes their asses fat
and their tits supple to ticklish.

Shit, it could be anything,
these women appear genetically modified
bodily farmed

bodily coded
and naturally signifying the cultural apparatus.

On the one hand,
my restraint is purely prudential—
there are no secrets any longer.

Sade had his dungeon.

There are too many people now.
Communication is too good
too strong.

On the other hand,
if she's old enough to call my name against my will
then she *may* be old enough for me. 18 is still too young.

The generality with which the legal sphere
understands me,
keeps me from approaching everyday life
using my sense organs
trained only by their own spontaneous activity.
The norm is beyond the *alea*—
and tear gasses me
before ever making it to the anomic,
before there is the violence of the repression.
The morality of appearances
whose efficacious art of equity,
with its punishment, loss of social standing,
is a better policeman—
considering how the other-directed
censors thought
that can only conceive of itself,
only have a self-image,
by measuring its equivalence

to other players' in the network.

She'll be older later,
here and now I'm still untouched
needing to be touched.

This kind of isolation
makes the mind wander to the Impossible.

63. Judas

The only good thing I did for you
besides bend you from your linearity
is lead you to him.
I carry the luck,

the shame that makes you counter-gift to the opposite,

the hurt that educates
but demands a counter-transference,

the instability that leaves much to be desired.

I was Judas all along.
Everyone hates him.
He's the fool,
the devil thinking he's playing the lead
but having only a secondary existence,
one who's work is estranged,
benefiting the other, Him, never itself.

You always told me about the importance of Judas.
You even said he was your favorite once.

But fuck Judas

and fuck ME too, right?

I should've never said I was a Satanist.

But I got hemmed up in a personalized joke.

I made myself into a riddle,
but morphed into a joke,
swallowed up by the Unconscious—the Medium itself—

or maybe it was you, I don't know,
you always aspired to be the Medium,
loved God
wanted to Die to become Whole, a Contradiction,
but for now, you're just a message
that *I interpret* as best I can.

And if you look for signs,
you reduce God to His messages.

64. No better expression

Nothing better expresses my condition
than the opportunities one corporation gives me
to blatantly celebrate my apparently juvenile poverty
with the champagne of beers.

The 'freedom' of the rock bottom,
the life bare enough

to be negatively 'free' from private property—

the poor drink lower
than the *fashionably, mystically cheap.*

65. A farewell to magic

You hugged me with only one arm—just a hug
that didn't seduce my artificially childish corpse
to transfigure it with intentions.

You hugged me goodbye
and I didn't imagine it and it finally sank in
with the addition of your butterfly-like weight:
convention or reality
was no longer parasitized or pasteurized
by the poetic or the philosophic.

In retrospect,
the straightforward sensations
of moving your bathing suit,
taking for granted the benefits of thumbs,
to see your tattoo,

of touching your elastic back to better see the blemishes.

The sensations
weren't of the jeopardized form
that must be answered with questions
for the sake of originality
that itself is only a product of the demand to separate.

66. A good first impression

The sunscreen makes a skin-tight biosphere
with a protective metaphysic
that falls short of philosophy,
closer to the micro-management of everyday life
by the bizarre,
and shocks me into endurance of an unbearable reality
that exhausts and equilibrates me.

But we got burned together
and drunk
and laughed
and didn't complain about anything
with joys that have overcome optimism
and sorrows that have overcome pessimism
and a mystery about something
that could potentially occur once
and still etch itself
into this glacial, Mediterranean servitude
of almost numerological immediacy
into the heart, not just the mind
for want of a praxis that takes no samples
and doesn't argue.

There was something about that lucidity
of a simple interaction
that wasn't hyper-conscious—
neither unlimited nor restrictive, but selective,
never unfair for not being universal or petty,
for not being partial.
Something to which there was no systematicity
almost made one believe in Nature,
if only it too was a legitimate mystery
and *unmotivated* attractor.

67. Outside of work

Your highlights were looking like the commercial

and that is rarer than an object
that defies sense but lets itself be known.

And whatever simply lives up to itself
has a miraculous quality, today.

There was nothing confusing about your hair
or the bridge of your nose
or your chin
or the splotches on your skin
the doctors couldn't diagnose
or your alien emoji tattoo,

and that kind of critique of the conceptual
makes me ascend to my own species.

When the apple fell on Newton,
he quickly jumped to Force itself,
but when you fell to me,
I was faced with The Situation.

When the bare is frosted
by the concrete at its foundations,
the contingents lack the terror of the alien.

68. You and me materially

There's nothing metaphysical about sitting with you
and we never talk shit
just to have something to say

or when you do, I try to redirect you to aporia.

That *something to say* is a pressure.

And there's nothing 'interactive' about our relations,
we never talk about culture
politics
or television.
I do, but you just giggle and punch me in the arm.

Thankfully, the internet can be the void
that sucks the filler from the everyday into its flat chasm.
Our mouths will be free for eating together
drinking together
and resting in a silence that just feels right.
So, we will also give the world a rest,
even if it won't take it.

That *something to talk about* is a distraction
from all the brute facts of our contiguity
like the contiguity of the stop sign and the yield sign.

The sound of your butt against the wet lounge chair
of the housewives complaining and praising
of wet feet slapping against the pavement
hotter than a motherboard getting digitized
and the sounds of the gang of children
swimming in the adult pool
during adult swim in the other.

This kind of sobriety is never dull.
There is nothing marvelous.
The colloquial will make me average
and knowledgeable:
you and I and life at its most basic from the inside out.

69. Don't put this meeting to effective use fellow human

I've already learned that conditions can appear
and not only appear, feel perfect
and still nothing might happen.
You're the type to sabotage.
Me too.
Maybe you'll bend it on itself
and I'll bend it on itself
and it will end up straight.

I'm an able-bodied
highly-intelligent
90-something-percentile type
they tell me
when I succeed their successes and fail their failures
and you can see what I've done
with my personal freedom
and my personal responsibility
whether on purpose or by chance
freely or passively or accidentally
or at the hands of some evil demon.
If I can't blame anyone else, I can't blame myself,
and if I can't blame myself, I can't blame God.

I'm the one they want:
the good-looking, well-raised, socially-relevant,
make-the-crowd-laugh-in-the-interview,
sell-lots-of-merch,
affluent-white-male type,
but I didn't want any of it,
didn't have time for it,
wasn't about to put the effort in.
So, I ruined all that with unsuccess
and gained the growing-pace of a plant
that needs minimal sun and attention.

I 'wasted' my education on philosophy
with which I can do nothing.
I have enough poems to publish books,
but no,
no poems published, not yet.
I'm working a mediocre profession anyone could do
living somewhere anyone could live,
mediocre or worse,
populated by mediocre or worse people
that are not specific to the area.
I'm overqualified for my job,
so are most human beings.
I'm dissatisfied with my environment, who wouldn't be?
I'm not blaming,
but sometimes on bad days
I'm imaginarily murdering the 'local population'
for their petty, private bullshit
that spills over into 'public life',
anyone with a need to live
and the knowledge that others must share that
would.

What is the goal?
They're asking me what the goal is.
Do I want to become a manager,
do I want to move up higher than that?

I've started small.
I think life is long,
it's only short when you cut it up into moments
even if those moments, like poems, stretch time
making it appear longer
slower
timelier than the straightforward.
It's always the "life is short" types

who speed through their lives,
the segmented moments of which
are like the lane dividers on the road
signifying a passing zone.
The 'substantial' majority of time is not a moment,
and it too is lived.
I'm on my way somewhere I'm setting myself up for.
I keep it a secret
because if someone knew, including me,
they could stop me.
But I'm moving, I have been this whole time,
never stopped.
The little goals I live me every day make me an art:
my art
society's art
humanity's art
the world's art.
And I get good friends out of my ambiguity
since I only attract those who have unlearned good faith
and have become habituated to suspension of judgment,
daring ones.
You've given me time.
I hope that it's nothing intangible.
I hope that it's *not just* the vibe
or the common interest in the avoidances
of alcohol and smokes.
I hope it's the human I have become,
didn't have to become—the beauty of the labor.
You're friendly to everyone,
so I'd never know,
and you'd never express how much
or what you like about hanging with me.

But listen, if we're hanging
then it can't remain desirable
unless it's suitable to the future

insofar as avoidances are valuable
only if they congeal
as *potential raw material* for future creativity,
that idleness of bodies,
aloofness of minds about to leap—

don't worry about the future.
You're on your way somewhere.
It's a secret.
I won't ask,
and if I find out, I won't tell you and ruin it for you.
You're an avoider.
You avoided something once,
avoided the consequences *of the avoidance*,
but you'll get over that by avoiding it somehow.

You say they always want something,
and they do.
I know.
Believe it or not, they have been either mystified by
or all too certain of me,
relating to social representations that filter me out.
They'll do it again if you don't get in the way.

But consider how I might respect you
and admire you
and write poems about you *already*,
while you're no one at all,
seeing you do everyday things with everyday people
before you have a career
or a degree
or 1001 nights of adventure.

70. only the boss gets married

She put a note in my back pocket
that said "IM SO SO SOO in love with you."
They're all so horny
lonely
their words mean little
with the excessiveness
of their being used in contradictory cases.
They are as dramatic as the next episode
according to the end of this episode
which is already last episode before it finishes.

She was 18
looked 15
acted whatever the age of the eternal feminine is—
ageless
forever young or immediately aged and calculated.

Every time I'm weak
dying
exhausted and in pure flight,
they come with sudden memories and words
like grave-robbers reaching into the surface
under which feelings exist
that no longer have anything to relate to
because their symbolic order
was the fashion of a day
that has by now gone.

Every time the sad eyes come out
like flowers that miss the earth,
they come pitiably
and like greater masters, I fall for their old shitbox
because I feel bad.
Already weak,

I feel that Christian pity
and the sorrowful feelings start to become blessed
and I hop from floor that's caving in
to floor that's caving in.
I'm avoiding everything seismically.
Everything works, but only partially
as a system
a crazed, fucked up system
of items that don't go together, but all function together,
that switch like watch-guards
circling around the sickbay, bored,
around a high-profile prisoner
in the grips of a serious illness.
Everything amongst everything
relating to everything
like Xanax relates to Cocaine.
The cycle, I'm flushing my life down—
shit-cycling all my pain.
I have psychological AIDS.
I'm a pussy,
but a pussy too dry
too shallow
to get fucked hard.

Everyday life hasn't caught up yet.
I'm writing the poetry.
The poetry should be dead by now.
This won't get published,
who's going to read this?
I'm at the end of it,

but wouldn't that be beautiful.

The human race would be young again,
but not romantic young—
a youthfulness that underneath it all

mistrusts, tests and feels.
I can only hope
the need for poetry will perish from this earth
and there will be creatures
that won't even curse its name,
especially not in the name of some other narcotic.

For now,
I'll try not to.

71. The miracle

The 'miracle' of genius develops
spirals slowly
drifts invisibly
in the guts
in the minutiae
the raw material of the average lives
lived by average people.

It is not in exceptional moments
that the poetry comes,
it's not in moments special to special people
it's not in superhuman moments
but in average times undergone a million times
by a billion people.

Warhol's snobby diary
him alone at the grocery store isn't interesting

and not because the grocery store isn't interesting.

Of course,
only a snob could give the credit to the art object itself—

a problem for art.

72. Shitting bricks

The satisfaction is partial
and desire aims only at desire
and products aim only to be bought
and holes aim only to be fucked
or receive satellites that relay information
with a voluntary entropy,
but the people aim for nothing.

Life takes work,
the shit work turns them against work itself,
choosing desire over need,
sacrificing need to buy shit,
good looking shit
designed by the genius of the consumer's dreams
and a lab tech
who doesn't flush for himself the shit he makes.

The thought does not have time to develop,
so it doesn't.
The fat cells stick together but contribute nothing,
and not even on purpose or by design.
And the fit bots are factory farmed
with artificially flavored security
and guaranteed resemblance,
but do more, so have more say
and turn their world that we also inhabit
into an obstacle course
that costs money but cannot be won
just 'enjoyed' at peak physicality

and acute positivity that numbs the nerves as a clean cut.

The mental gymnastics of the university
is noothing other than a collective discharge
of pure functionality.
The ideal functioning of the brain in scholarship.
The ideal functioning of rationality in economics.
The ideal functioning of the body in exercise.
The ideal functioning of the mucous membranes
in sex—

this ultimate wastage of a human life individually,
of a social life collectively,
of humanity historically.
But I'm no hippie, so litter all the used words
onto an otherwise pristine view
of un-concreted-over land!

73. The slippage of the craft

I don't have a choice but to work
and the work has my appetite too busy to eat,
as easily spooked as a gazelle at the water's edge.
I'm holding in my shits
in the trenches of this job,
crawling up the backs of others no matter what,
and I'm not even in the middle of the pile,
I'm closer to the wall—
pulling people up with me
like the plastic monkey at the top of the barrel.

They won't respond to negativity,
blatantly,
with the convenience of ignorance

and the power of the middle man
to silence their one talent—
the right to say nothing,
the 5th dimension—
and they're filling their cheerleaders
with one-at-a-time coins,
piggy-banking off their porcelain smiles
and then breaking them
and collecting their investments,
the only substance their followers had.

They only have the pensiveness of something pending
and they depend heavily on the working illusion
of the reality of the respect they demand monologically
with the effort of the Jews,
who themselves couldn't have built the pyramids
without the whip chapping their asses
until they swelled and became tender fetishes.

I'm the glue and the sticky bomb
keeping the other workers watching,
and the only energy left in this utopia of fabled bees
is the fallout of its implosion—
its vices.

They're telling us we can do more
be more
become more without drugs,
a montage that gaps up time,
steroids
or a nice numbing lube that relaxes the sphincter.
They're telling us everything is possible,
that we're talented but going to waste,
that you have to spend money to make money
and maybe they believe themselves
and maybe not,

but they're worth money and they pray.

They need God
and their God doesn't need them
and they know it,
so they nag Him
with friend requests He never responds to
but cannot eliminate.

They always get their way
because their way is whatever exists,
they aren't picky,
but whatever they choose is called the 'high standard'.
They are "tough but fair"
and that "but" is one of reluctance
even if they speak as lightly as a lamb.

I'm not their rival.
If I fuck them from the inside
it's because I'm too fascinated by their stupidity
to intervene in their downward spiral.
I ride this top-down society
like a convertible
that ruins my hair and chaps my skin,
but makes me stop caring about any of its affectations.

74. When comes

The hawks do no look fearsome, they appear normal
and unworthy of my wonder,
and the plants that cannot uphold their own weight
droop down like bodies that look like bags
holding but not bracing limp, tangley bodies
like water hoses

that become mythical for the offspring of the laborer.

Women make gravity dully haughty and expected.

The black people are welcoming
even when you cannot tell
if they are angered or thoroughly enjoying themselves
because their voices carry
because they carry on
with the strange endurance of the invisible,
and I even enjoy when they talk during the film.
Their voices sound wittier,
having been silenced for an unimportant length.

The women give me their pain
and I write it down,
striving for a plastered justice
that neither nature
nor art nor history nor consumption seem to give.
They stand naked before me
like trees no one measures the history of
because they seem timeless
trees with all the bottom limbs cut off
that are lush at the top,
and I can't see what's up there without an apparatus,
and even with one, I can't isolate which tree they are,
whereas I remember them individually
in terms of their difference
from the breakage of each trunk
that allows me to move in and out of their shade,
so I can see them from as many perspectives
as they permit.

75. Drew Carey

Drew Carey reminds me
that the apocalypse is a real thing,
that it happened already
and left no traces of its liposucked crime,
and like an abusive partner has you convinced to this day
that it's some insufficiency in your actions
sucking out the joy but not gargling it in front of them
in a way pleasurable to them.

I still don't know the difference
between Price Is Right and Let's Make a Deal.
This liminal flamboyance
between morning and lunchtime(?)
displays itself with exactitude:
America's interpretation
of Japan's interpretation
of American capitalism.

I watch this show and think
"Who the fuck can place responsibility anymore?"

This wonderful governance
shares with us all the responsibility *only it believes in*
throughout a hellish deferral
founded upon a constant preemptive blackmail.

76. Existential crisis

What does this phrase mean today?
"Existential crisis" is having itself.

It has become too easy

to interpret something as an existential crisis
for there to be a thing, "existential crisis."

The demarcation of the qualitative criteria
for an existential crisis
sounds itself like a crisis-provoking critique.

People always in a crisis
make a language out of chattering teeth
that are more upbeat at a higher tempo than a heartbeat.

It used to only demand "Applause."
The world seems a giant teleprompter
for "Existential Crisis."
The materialists made sure to prove their ideology
by installing it into their transformed world.
The workers built their alienation and obsolescence
into the products.
The sexually repressed neuroscientist nerds
make the world a brain,
a big soft machine that stimulates itself
for a quick buzz—
a brain that is already a digital model of itself,
a brain that navigates itself via Google Maps
(readymade proof of the naturalness of the computer).

We are all bachelor machines
soliciting love with signs of critical demand
on this kiss-cam anachronistically called "Existence,"
each a response away from committing
in-demand, non-violent terrorisms
and feeling up for ourselves these crowdsurfing traumas.

77. the software

When you finally learn
who's moving the Ouija board,
it's already said and done.

78. the melodrama of proximity

how to burn off a tattoo→
why the Illuminati killed Robin Williams→
what they're really telling us during the Super bowl→
Lady Gaga the shapeshifting alien→
the Leipzig Connection→
former vampire speaks out→
the truth about Millennials→
eyebrow tutorial…

The internet is a stupid question

and a Response
never quite becomes an Answer.

79. commerciality

The integrated circuit
of a constant perspectival shift
cannot be separated
from the pathological passivity
of the viewer,
who is always-already one step behind
even the cameraman—

a higher order complicity
that is studious
and yet has grown to accept the vertiginous ambiguity
of everyday life
as reflected
in the circulation of the camera around its 'subject',
broken up by cut shots
like the programming
by the commerce it serves to apologize
with discontinuous technique.

80. Continuity

The personal can dramatize
explode
and culminate in murder or suicide.
The impersonal can cantankerously and tangentially
spill its contents socially.

On their own,
they are non-threatening,
each of them an irregular common sense.

But no one says anything
when the personal
becomes the impersonal.

81. Crime scene photos

The photographs I take always seem to me
to have the character of criminality
as if were one object removed

the whole edifice of the evidence would be spirited
away.
Of course, the crime scene exists
only because something is missing:
life
motive
the suspect.
The victim is there but not there,
the evidence is there but untampered with and
untouchable
and the criminal leaves only traces.

The crime scene focuses the retrospective gaze to the
victim
or the instruments of his victimization
as if the whole scene
and each lifeless object
that somehow appears deader and more indifferent
than in everyday life
as if it wanted to be sad but could only muster crocodile
tears.
The facticity of the photographs never evokes sorrow
but pure inspection
that stops just shy of becoming a lapse—
one observes its contours
as if participating in an experiment
that tests memory by taking something away
after giving the subject a set amount of time
to memorize it
who doesn't know what aspects they are to recall.
The photograph,
like everyday life,
is simultaneously an utter bore
(for the dead are complete beings
Perfections
that can only get revenge on the living with objectivity)

and clarified to the point that the eyes grow restless
and out of habit scan the scene as if seeing a commercial
who's constant perspectival shift
is more effective than the message.

The objects in the photographs
only perpetuate the victim's death
as if they are already in the cellophane
with DNA that isn't yet comprised by touch.
They reflect a nefarious lack of physicality
as if they only overcome their neglect
by microscopic scrutiny.
And best of all, they lose their glamor
as the human body, by being surrounded,
produces an effect of over-proximity
and the objects become as numerous and systematic
as they are.

And yet the poetic
really over-dramatizes this rather calm
and safely extenuated viewer experience—
and it is over before you know it
just like the wandering mind
shelled in everyday
by ubiquity.

82. The cell door opens

The women are no longer
the kitchen slaves they once were.
Now they work to buy the food.
And yet now
we are all, men, women, trans, queer, etc., alike
more dependent on the food industry,

and thus hungrier,
than ever.

83. "The whites are innocent in their guiltiness," said the
    white

> Scrawny teenage forgettables
> with wispy arms and fat pockets
> stretched out along the hand-me-down line
> and hacked prescriptions to the porn
> that teaches your chalky daughters
> how to fuck with an open throat
> no words
> and a desire to be raped
> that will put black men in jail who turn them down.
> Pale insomniacs with blue lips
> and nothing but search engines and a shitty connection
> will make pipe bombs
> once the water has been shut off
> because the heroin lifted from the evidence room
> that their parents bought
> doesn't pay the bills.
>
> White blonde filter-feeders
> raised in the area of the white man's Diaspora
> from "the ghetto blacks" their economics created
> intending to keep their daughters' cherries BBC free
> who are twerking in the front yard
> doing crotch crease yoga
> as practice for the Tinder profile
> groups of five
> ten
> twenty
> white girls

whose insurance will eventually pay for Botox
and reconstructive surgery,
for titjobs gone awry,
who will touch black women's hair
like squishy toys in their salt-water pools
on repossessed land
their parents bought cheap at the auction,
whose thriftiness will make them reality stars
in their ivory tax bracket.

Little white blonde nothings
raised by old white blonde nothings
whose deaths are hidden by dead whales
and monkeys with severed skulls
and brains drying from the lube
and rats as clean as the bathroom sink they refuse to use
because of the human intervention in its cleanliness,
preferring to use the sanitizer on the exit door,
doing the manager a favor
and letting him know when its empty.
Old white women in Q3 of their lives
who still look shocked at the Asians
Indians
Middle Easterners renting their husbands' real estate
because the old KK town has the best schools.
Old white blonde nothings
who will say "excuse me" rudely
and get offended if you react rudely
because they used the words,
who'll honk in the McDonald's drive-through line
and get free meals due to their distaste
and have picnics with wine
at all-white country music festivals
that raise money for white charities,
forgetting that country comes from the blues,
unaware where the blues come from

because of the memories white guilt has redacted
while their daughters are home
juicing up their cherries
with BBC unable to rape them from the computer
during their primitive fantasies.

Let the families of the murdered
the gypsies
the "sand niggers"
the slingers
the policed
the parked trailers
whites with PTSD become the unemployable of the
military
the failed SAT scores without tutors
the bullied
those who get arrested with their rich friends
who get bailed out immediately
and blame them for their cop-attracting poverty—
let the octopus-armed Latinos in the open kitchens
reduced by Disney to talking kitchen instruments
the little white girls can play with
while they learn
and prepare for their slave-owning futures—
let the "faggots"
and landscapers
the garbage men
reported by residents for bending the cans,
those who sleep through their educations
because they babysit
while Mr. mom works the third shift—
let them splatter paint
the only colorful parts of the whites' bodies
the entrails
the undigested kale
the Mexican coke

the blood updated with yearly vaccines,
paint their doughy bodies
all over the cookie cutter houses
until the prices drop so low
not even the white lesbians will take the steal deal.

84. For my unpublished love

Having twice thought I was truly in love
it was only fear of being alone
for to ignore the question "how to live"
and defer the answer with the overblown.

Having always cast contemptuous eyes
and accused the other of conspiratory lies,
I've never taken responsibility
that such distractions bless my instability.

With former company I have consumed,
I deadened my sense to that chill in the room
that I've never learned how to really love
with never a clue why it's two turtle doves.

Your heart is only matched by your effort
and to wake up to your curlers was magic,
to see the you you kept private and covert
with me as the one you let witness and have it.

You never loved me for my art
nor my manner of sounding smart.
I never thought someone could love *my* favorite
who existed much longer than the behavior did.

You loved the goodness not many see

that I swallowed and chased with Hennessy.
I ignored how consistently old "me" welled up
with you there to keep calling bad-me's bluff.

The truth always has been that I'm a sap
that no one would ever appreciate,
who, more into the mysteries, the evil, the hate,
made me fall dopily into their trap.

And how ridiculously you were accused
when *you* could still love after being abused,
which I refused to consider, perhaps as jealous
as the dirt at the ivy climbing the trellis.

And to think that I could have killed that part
of you, whose feelings (like mine once) were art—
thinking that jabbering philosophy made the man
with a dissociation that missed your circuited tram.

With love for the dimpled smile at that horrible job,
I miss the clutter for which I called you a slob.
How I invaded your space and policed you in it,
which you told me you hated because others did it.

I am smart enough to have learned and listened,
but always interrupted with *my* dreams and wishes.
And how my compensations were such small beer
when even they were *for me, my* rules & *my* cheer.

You taught me better than anyone could
how strongly my self clang to the misunderstood
to perpetuate an inherited desire to control
that made it always think it was on a roll.

How I yelled at you at the birthday party
you threw for me like no one ever has,

especially those who've experienced the bad
of this ignorant, bitter, unappreciative smarty.

My past made you cut me some slack
until the washed-out cycle made you react
and become the very worst part of yourself
that was better left on your inner shelf.

But how I admire your strength to overcome
that to which weaklings like me would've succumb.
I've never had this respect for another.
Not myself, my professors, my therapist, my mother.

And I'm not sure what frightens me more—
that I lost you for good by being a whore,
by blaming you for my bad habits 'you worsened'
or that you're my soul mate, my rock, my person.

I can only hope that one day you'll know
the "me" that you inspired me to create and to grow,
the me that's in love with you enough to stay
cautiously, considerately, attentively away

with hopes of returning to see you succeed
without the former me to beg, cry and plead,
who may not believe in the religious marriage
but who believes in YOU, his pumpkin carriage.

85. I got woes in different area codes

I'm a life-ruiner,
so it only makes sense that I'm a vacation-ruiner.
I'm trying to seclude myself.
No matter how sad I am,

I don't want my sadness to affect the people.
I'm ruining people's family beach portraits
with my woes,
but I cut back from the hard sand where the water is
to the soft sand
to get out of their shots.
There is magic all around me, probably.
People say that.
David Foster Wallace said that before he killed himself
and my books are as long as his is,
so I should probably be worried.
There is beautiful, everyday human life all around me,
but I won't recognize it.
I can't.
It would kill me if I did.
I have to feel nothing to live.
The drugs booze sex cigarettes
worked better than what the doctor gave me,
but they ruined everything good I had
and gave me these blues I chose over her.
The people on the beach are ignoring me,
and I'm glad
because that means they don't have these blues
don't understand these blues
don't have the time or patience for these blues.
I'm comparing myself to everyone
to them
to my desires
to who I want to be
or used to be but smashed to bits
to get over the blues
that threatened that person's existence.
I had to leave each me behind with each heartbreak.
I'm running out of new people to be
and each new person repeats what the old person did,
anyway.

There are children digging holes in the sand
deep enough to bury me.
There are hideous birds with one leg
that seem to fair better than me.
I see the obese people in two pieces
who seem pleasantly pleasured.
The abuelas recognize this look on my face.
The ukuleles are offensive to these blues.
The black families just remind me of her.
She isn't responding to the dead gestures I leave
at her doorstep
like a cat leaving rodents for its master
in brief moments when it isn't indifferent
like they say.

She's moving to another state
and I'm never going to see her again.
One of the last things she said to me
was I'm pathetic and she feels sorry for me.
I'm worried these blues will only attract another woman
who my mother loves
who will fall in love with my sadness
make me happy
then leave when the job is done
to start the whole process over again.

I'm walking under mobs of the gulls
and they are not shitting on my head,
but these blues trick me into calling it a fortune.
They say love is for the birds.
More like a Twitter bot
that follows me and gets me excited
but unfollows me
when my account is inactive.

86. The nursery rhyme consciousness

They repeat what the media says
what the coloring books say
what the Bible says on the back of the cereal box.
They inject their meaning into the entire world order
and back pedal
when the contradictions are acknowledged
when the murder of brown people
of rationality
of argument is acknowledged,
not even when their misunderstanding
of the history of their religion is acknowledged.
If you make a good point,
because they forgot to interrupt you,
it's time for them to go to bed.
There is a war against Christianity
carried out by Christianity.
Where the religion is deeply woven
into the fabric of the economy
and based on the stream of consciousness
of what is magical simply because it is uttered.
Anything could have been true
may be true in infinite possible worlds.
Everything is true at least in some possible world.

There is a war on Christianity in America.
Christianity didn't win—isn't still winning *without God.*
America wasn't the product of Christianity.
America wasn't built on slavery.
The Natives weren't slaughtered by Christianity.
Colonialism wasn't a product of Christianity.
Christianity didn't consider black people inferior
didn't take their language away
their habitus away

didn't take their mutilated body off the Levi's Jeans logo
to cover its tracks.

These women—
who believe their All-Mighty God
their Beginning and End
is in a war against Satan and will eventually win
BUT NOT YET, only when He feels like it—
are jabbering like the dirt bikes
in the ring of death,
that spherical cage
where three daredevils circle each other at high speeds
with I want to say fire somehow involved,
but I'm too exhausted
after this Jackson Pollock discussion,
for which the increase in price is somehow unlimited,
to integrate it imaginatively.

And somehow doing cocaine is a sin.

87. The racket of the earth

They look at the gentrified commercialism
of the beach towns without hippies
and say, "At least they have trees."
They jabber on about the sweetness of the margarita
for longer than it takes to fuck or shit.
They get excited about ferns growing off trees.
They get Beatlemania over 2 seconds of dolphin fins
and their phones, unlike their minds
hearts
genitals,
are on continuous autofocus.
They buy white houses

with white fences
that keep their white SUVS safely contained
within the sphincter of their driveway
and marry white
buy white
fuck and suck white.
Their circles of friends
are roundabouts that eliminate stop signs
with a "get in where you fit in" norm.
Their smiles age them.
They equate walking with the Old Testament
and rent casual bikes that lift and shape the buttocks.
The lines on and the arrows
and the crosswalks on the road
are all white
because that which is good for you,
directs you and keeps you safe
is white.
The speed limit signs are white,
but the posted speed is black
because the thing that you want to break,
the thing that oppresses you,
the thing that you don't believe in
is black.
The asphalt, that which reflects heat and ruins the land
but on the back of which you travel
to get to your destination
is black.
That which is turned off is black,
that which disrupts the social and the sight and message
is black.

Of course, death rode a white horse.

88. Community

The political subjects
form communities and localities
to combat globalization and integral publicity,
but they are private communities
like the gated neighborhoods they scoff at
from their private vehicles
to their own personalized playlists.

89. Indecent Exposure

The indecency
of a poet's marketing strategy and SEO
will expose the repetitive nature of his poetry
that ceases to *act*
when it *applies* the common consensus.

And yet my poetry can *repeat repetition*
and still be more valuable
in the play on simulation.

90. Petsmart

She knows how to get what she wants
by letting people talk for her,
she's pet smart...

like most attractive or successful people.

91. Hostage-taking vagueness

The abandoners *TELL YOU*
that *words mean nothing to them*
and become abusive—
their pacifying, apoplectic inheritance—
when you don't listen.

92. How I will remember her

Touted
ambition
suspends
happy
identity.

93. 'Non-profit'

She loathes work
and thus the creature that she is
and aims only at consequences,
the most coveted of which, for her and others, is rest—
the feeble-mind, near-sighted contentment of old age
terminated by its namesakes,
in which a small fraction of life is free,
and the very worst fraction at that,
having reached its tipping point earlier than its death.

They cannot work without tax-free compassion
that supposedly blesses their conscience,
having only worked because they are made to.

They are wedded to their work
that to them is a waste if others do not value it,
if others are not engaged in the same type of work,
and they only do this as the lesser of all evils.

They enjoy working for others.
They live to serve.
And her guru recruited her *from the service sector*,
his loyal field slave he brought into his house.

She told me not to give up my vision
as if I needed to need reassurance,
as if I needed to have my feet washed,
and yet all her projects are collaborative—
diluted through the sieve of the overwhelming consensus
and the approval of investors.

I told her she was going to get sucked up
into the dizzying whirl of the rich,
who cannot live without being heroes
ego-boosted by humility,
who trade money with each other to avoid taxes
and *reform* only small segments
of the world they are *partial* to,
listening to each other speak about what drives *them*
why it drives them
why it should drive others.
They cannot believe
unless they can share their beliefs,
so unconfident
they must inspire others to believe.
They are influencers—the innovative word for moralists
whose self-interpretations must involve the sizzle-words
of the menus of touristy cafes.
There is an overwhelming desire
to show irrefutable proof,

sometimes in the form of 90-minute movies
of the importance of their work,
as satisfied as dogmatic logicians at metalanguage,
at the go-aheads
of awesomeness they fish for from their admirers
willing to bite without bait.

She said love never works out for her,
but she said I love you first,
and when *she decided* when it *didn't* work out,
she invoked Reality.
But she only believed in a customary love.
When it failed (*which determined future failures*),
she stopped believing in it
because she never chose any of her values
and yet had no metanarrative to ground her values.
She loses love as if Love has failed,
like something has been expropriated.
And she turns against what was supposedly *her* value
as if all love is false.
Her love is 'non-profit'
and thus in constant crisis
and interminable, Absolute failure,
as surely as loving thy neighbor as thy self is impossible.
The Same as a constant flight from self
that causes a devaluation of the human itself.
Never self-overcoming…
the desolation of self-actualization.

94. Bachelor in Paradise

The redundancy of each new getting-to-know
differentiates with homogenous intensity
and what hurts most *distinctively*

is that all the secrets they shared
will have become common knowledge,
and there is nothing poetic about that obscenity.
And if I wasn't the only *one* around
when you needed *someone*
I wouldn't have gotten the final rose.

I am drowning in the overavailability
of what I don't need.

95. *Please* pay

The state parks function on the honor system
with no one to collect the entry fee,
and everyone still rushes to pay
when no one is around
as if scrambling to pay at the highway toll
with a line of cars behind them—
the time before honesty became lie.

96. Nice

They're nice.
That means they're agreeable,
which means they're obedient.

Could also mean
they just like you like an equal.

And unless you respect them,
you consider both motivations repugnant.

97. Multiple levels at once

The people
and the businesses
and governments are the same.
You plead with them not to do something
and you provide reasons that appeal to your needs
and what affects you
and how you are/were affected by it/
how you will be affected
if it happens to you again by their hand,
and they do it anyway
as if you gave them the idea
and are to blame for their reaction.
The people
businesses
governments are the same.
They use your biggest fears
they made you feel comfortable enough to confess
and use them against you as blackmail
to hold you hostage
and to determine the norm of the relationship.
The people
businesses
governments
all the same.
They pressure you into romantic relations
when you weren't ready
to be anything other than friends
and by the time they make you trust them enough
to be with them,
they withdraw their sidereal love,
but want to be friends—
knowing you can't withdraw your love as quickly,
holding you love hostage,
trying to make love with you

when you're with someone else,
telling you they love you,
miss making love with you
and yet accuse you of pressuring them
when you stand up for yourself.
The people
businesses
governments
all same,
peddling freeware,
waiting until you become dependent on their services,
then charging by the month
for the rights to use their product
that you cannot be successful without in this economy
telling you they still love you after its over
and accusing your love of being false
when you forget them to move on
and to function healthily.
The people
business governments
same,
providing security but creating a projected insecurity
and constructed ambiguity,
abandoning you for a career
that provides more in its transitory metempsychosis
than your loyalty.
The people the same
businesses the same
governments the same,
issuing vague directives that imply no depth
and provoke no contemplation
via reflexive signals that communicate nothing,
and when you break these ambiguous rules,
they convince you that you don't listen,
that you're a selfish, shit listener
as if clarity and cogency

is whatever they determine it is—
because they are so embedded in your consciousness,
you should be reading their minds.
The people and the governments and the businesses
convince you
they don't need you but you need them,
telling that you'll be back
no matter how much you hate them,
daring you to ghost them as if you will always be empty,
as if they will be the first and only memory
you will ever retain—the doctor—
having intentionally forgotten all the others
as if your affinity for them wasn't elective,
as if your love can't form a hierarchy
with a base you invented yourself
given what has been done to you,
telling you they pity you
because you were pathetic
to have opened yourself up to them in the first place,

blaming their abuse on you.

98. Softcore slavery

The whites are speaking for the blacks
the men for the women
the rational for the irrational
the straight for the queer
the rich for the poor
the blacks and the women and the queers for oppression
the one for the many
the many for the individual
the media for the event.

Not sure if it was the beatings
or if it's the bystander effect,
but when I see someone unconscious—
paralyzed and thus not suffering—
I move slowly
as if they are faking it,
maybe I'm denied death-sensitivity
by the 24-hour obituary reel
for people
ideas
techniques
and models.

The job is fucking my creativity.
The credit has me ahead of myself working to catch
up—a perfect alibi

The success stories
are of the ones who stretched themselves early
with butt plugs of graduating circumferences
who don't feel it as much when it slides in unopposed.
Capitalism shields us in a wet, *white* tee shirt
with erect nipples from the cold that simulate pleasure.

Our abuser capitalizes on its cowardice,
apologizes for the beating
but makes sure we know how easily it could've killed
us,
how thankful we should be.

And our abuser—
tougher than all women combined and yet feminine—
fears *our* death that reflects its failure and needs us to
need it

and I see my meager earnings

and my resentful condition
and the youthful neurotic resilience that's left me
reflected in a little cooler turned upside down
to drain the ice melt in the center of the lawn
where the sun hits rain beating its bottom
into grass sinking into its own secretions that have
hardened and accumulated over time

when all along the water adhering to its guts would have
gone on its own.

99. My stable ignorance

As the information spreads
and the words divide and conquer,
my ignorance remains unmoved and unchanged.

It never has to grow in power.
It grows in potential but does so automatically
and without any qualitative alteration.

As the internet grows—or time divorced from space—
my ignorance stays little,
since it never ignores bit by bit
(which is how the internet grows)
but all at once.

When you wrestle with demons,
the demons also grow stronger.
You have given them a strategy
to familiarize themselves with,
and you'll never win once and for all.

Sure, my ignorance didn't happen all at once.

But once it happened, it lasted.

100. Cliché

The only thing cliché-proof is a cliché.

Something cannot be made cliché that already is cliché.

Whatever is a mere repetition of itself
will lead others astray
who would have repeated it otherwise.

And yet—to a cliché, everything that isn't cliché
is boring.

101. One Life to Live is a daytime soap opera, a poem inspired by Stanley Kubrick

The pushy manliness,
that fatal strategy
the blowback of which is never calculated
or calculated only to the extent no one asks any questions,
that paranoid obsession
armed with the work ethic
of a naturalized master
that controls to the point of its own psychosis
to the point where every new creation and art
can be traced to the control,
where every possible perspective
becomes implicitly focused on the control,
where every current activity

is sacrificed to the maintenance of the control,
where every externality is ignored
for the closure of the effort expended
on the exponentially vanishing permanence
of the control,
the amiability of which
is that of a master saving the slaves from themselves
and their backwards ways.

This manliness couldn't exist
were something to have not already disappeared,
not so much an archaic privilege
as a former means to confidence
in a world whose control
consists precisely in the psychosis of its members
who harm one another
in attempt to regain what it *really has* taken from them,
while it never feels a thing
and controls evermore quietly
in each of its dedicated copycats
who'd rather act against their own best interests
than admit of the truth.

This pushy manliness
can be found in religion
in the megachurches
in politics
in the 24-hour independent news
in film
in the jarring provocations of the senses
of art-house
in music
in punk rock
in the automobile
in the self-driving car.
These already dead avenues,
these naked performance artists
trying to make the body reappear

as they hiss phonemic kegels of the throat,
are screaming in your face
BELIEVE IN ME
DON'T LOSE INTEREST
LOSING INTEREST IS DEATH
LOSING INTEREST IS DEFEAT
LOSING INTEREST IS DEATH.
Yes, even the punks
don't want your negativity or your loss of faith
and even the Marxists
want to keep their jobs by perpetuating a need for Marx,
from whose philosophy Amazon benefits the most.
All these elements
these solutions
these alternatives
these wishbones and suction-cupped dildos
these forms of insurance
that benefit from the creativity of your lies
and from your fear of insanity
or the loss of credibility
testimony
or social desirability,
essentially your fear of death
and the objective quality of the dead
that is all the stronger the deader you really are.

To face the reality of our world,
whose non secret depends on history's continuity
that only propels itself on its own inertia—
the no longer relevant all too relevant forms
that continue to signify a lack of spirit—
you would have to become insane
if it is insane to ignore the "thou shalt" in our happiness.

But you wouldn't want to be like me,
who no one wants to be around
as if I were death itself, the failure of all things.
The whole narrative

mined from the incautious atheists
that there is only one shot
that has blessed the neurosis of immediate pleasure
and a perpetual joke
that makes a watered-down seriousness
seem evermore real.
It is heretical to be alone
to be suspicious of happiness
and yet not be social enough to form a pessimistic ideology
and share burdens.
For the fun morality
is a lithium that prevents the need for restraints,
while the actual restraints are only symbols
to the demonstrators who imagine restraints
are still necessary,
for the domination
to still appear to be external.

102. The Critique of the environment

A child's finger can crush a thorax
like a grape
and the sky or the ocean
can make private property seem the hideous jewels
of a lost vessel, datable but beyond consciousness,
become the cultural inertia of a pseudoscience
of the senses
locked in the craggy display of a credible leisure zone
within a semi-private space.

103. The obvious, if stated, is suspicious

The horror is not so much

that you cannot function *like normal people*
that you cannot relate
to what they do 'healthily and freely'
without getting absorbed in it
collapsing with it
using and abusing it
obsessing over it
feeling smothered by it
detaching from it
from yourself through it
from reality with it
suffocating beneath it,
not really losing yourself in it
because there was no self before
because a self never congealed
with the parents' use and abuse regarding their marriage,
a little trap for my mom set by my dad
and a little excuse for my mom to leave my dad
and re-enter life,
my dad's detachment and suffocation
and my mom's obsession and absorption,
their mutual feeling of being smothered by me
and losing themselves in me
and their marriage collapsing because of all that.

Or what little self solidified
like a hairball coughed up by a cat that licked itself raw
was fractured once,
just before the little ball could descend
and accumulate more and more weight
simply because a momentum
has already been set in motion in a past,
the elevation of which is itself
the product of a long history of accumulation.
And before the fractured self
could reconstruct what few pieces it had,

those pieces were shattered again
by another friendly neighborhood atrocity
that no one believes because it isn't rape
(even though I'm always getting fucked against my will
by complete strangers or those closest to me)
or poverty
(even though the poverty of spirit is universal or not at
all)
or racism
(even though *my* whiteness is not even a race;
it is a sign of a lack of race
through the watered-down promiscuity of poor people
who fucked themselves out of their cultural slavery
into their biological slavery)
or war (although the only war left is all against all)
or sexism
(although capitalism is sexist against all sexes,
always playing both sides
and making both sides
comfortable with masturbating in front of each other).
It's as if my parents' disbelief in
mistrust of
and trivialization of
the magnitude to which my experiences wasted me
has placed itself
into the *merely hypothetical and perhaps illusory hearts*
of everyone around me,
as if their denial
of the small beer that is my pain
reflects an even greater denial
of the social and personal atrocities
they continue to accept socially and personally.

The horror
is not that of your own private dysfunctionality,
but rather that the hyperfunctionality

of the addict
the pervert
the obsessive
the psychotic
the loser
is the norm—
that normal people are sustained
by their own disappearance
through the unhealthy and the unfree
that they lighten up with their density
before they adapt to the cave with blindness
so the light cannot kill them
simply because they are forever removed from it.

The horror is that no one
can use these metered parking spaces
without ill health and unfreedom as presuppositions.

104. Rebound from the woes

It feels good sometimes
to overcome your own imagination
that internalizes and simulates to understand.
I'm at the golden mean
between mania that interrupts thought
with an overabundance of focal thoughts,
an over-engaged commerciality of passive thought,
and depression that repeats a single obsession,
a gif that recycles a single gesture
that never finishes itself—
constantly interrupted by its beginning.

I get excited when I see black people
on this beach whose population is as white as the sand

because your people are everywhere,
no matter how unwelcome,
and perhaps there are people like me
like us
everywhere, too, dying this same death.

The people aren't looking at the ocean
or me
or each other
or at books,
and the internet pervades, invades and precludes
this edge of the white world.
The people cannot enjoy this place,
themselves,
or their company anywhere without the drink.
The people are taking pictures of the expected,
of what they took last year to catalogue their deaths,
the years before *ad infinitum,*
and nothing breaks through.
The men are all fat
or swollen with protein shakes and meal-replacements
and the life-replacement
of this sun-screened simulacrum of the Oceanic.
The women's spines are piercing their backs
like agile fins,
and you could do limbo through their thighs
that push out toned, agile infants
that start the process over again
like the game after you feed it quarters,
the cum of the arcade.
Everyone is a family here.
Everyone my age or younger has kids.
Some of the moms seem to present themselves to me
like cats with their asses to the moon,
like if I came on the ground they'd suck it inside them
like hens—

my metabolically chiseled bod that hasn't lifted in years.
Boats are drifting along the shoreline
with effective billboards.

Today, I'm not ashamed they're looking at my scars
my tiger stripes
my markings that ward off predators and attract victims.
Today, I'm picturing you and I
with caramel-colored babies
with hair the whites can only touch and dream of,
holding them up above the waves
like a toast to the immortal order
that is too certain for time's worry—
breaking the symmetry
of this greenest of all other sides of the fence.

105. In plain language

In the future, I love you now.

106. Womanhood in the paranoid age

To transcend the masses,
she becomes a technician
to be the reign of mediocrity's *better half*—
that she 'intends' to rule patriarchy like its silent partner
its nagging wife who rules it
by making it dependent on her
and, like any power-obsessed mind,
forgets the blowback of co-dependency
or makes it inevitable with her salon logic.

By revolutionizing it,
she damns herself to consciousness—
which takes the place of thought.

Only a deprived *enthusiast* could enslave herself
to her freedom.

107. The counter-balance whose justice does not level

When you're dissatisfied
with all the wealth you've given your life for,
I'll be your naïve, careless hero
dashing in (connecting two terms) unshielded
as the money burns holes in your pockets,
and I'll *make* a dwelling out of old boxes
(that shield products)
to *play* what is their reality,
and we can laugh together at the energy we spend
on everything but ourselves—
because the self is too costly to produce
and takes too much investment for such little returns.

108. Saviors (on the conception of 'a New Medium')

With a martyr's Socratic grandeur,
she disguises her underlying disease
with the false health of modernization—
a body with no appetite that doesn't sleep,
constantly agitated by its own resistance
to continuous production
and further toxified by stimulates.
She aims at reviving poetry

from its oversaturated banalization
by *forcing* it into her innovative product
(i.e., by cutting out the options),
in which the metaphors themselves are surveilled,
accumulating as data
that links up each poem to others
and suggesting that they be buddies
and collab
like the Lil Rascals climbing atop each other's shoulders
to fill out a grown man's suit.
Each poet saved and given an equal opportunity
by weighted variables
that limit or streamline users' preferential judgment.
Each poem saved
by being linked elbow to elbow to all other poems
'that *do the same things*
because *they use the same words.*'

She learned best from the Church
that to save something you must destroy it
(or to destroy something you must save it)—
Christianity founded on the death of Christ.
But she 'saves' poetry by putting it under a microscope
and studying the life out of it.
And perhaps poetry's suicide
will never have greater force
than when uploaded into a *living database*
that even Hegel would have found base.

She will save 'poetry' by destroying poiesis.
AND HER SHITTY POETRY
WILL BENEFIT THE MOST.
Because she can only conceive of herself
by ruining selfhood for everyone else,
can only speak by interrupting everyone else,
can only argue

by interpreting every contrary as complimentary—
winning by exhausting the 'listener' into agreement,
completely socially removed
and thus unable to pick up on bodily clues
that to someone normal would speak volumes
to how checked-out they are.

Thank God for my innocence
that might create something other than itself
for only thinking of the world thinking it.

She can only conceive of the Internet.

109. Keeping her without restricting her

Everyone everywhere looks up at her
like at a crystal chandelier
that sparsely yet completely illuminates
the people in the foyer,
like the mirror on the ceiling above the bed,
like a hidden camera on their anniversary.

Everyone hears her sing
and pushes her to value it by giving it meaning,
the meaning of which is but a trite social connotation
that ruins the gift in an economic operation
that people hope to steal
by accumulating her songs
that eliminate the action she enjoys
every time she gives form to her words.

Everyone looks at her in awe
and disgusts her by making her *a thing*
that shields them from their anxious freedom

and the tragedy of life *that doesn't work out*
(i.e., produce a fixity of *the age*).
Everyone wants something from her,
and by asking, ignores her interiority
and interrupts the voice that no one listens to.

I think what made her love me
was that I never made her signify
that I never made her a value,
which, again, would mean to *apply* to her
another trite social connotation
that completely missed the point *by making one*.
I never restricted her *to what she is*—
what always means *what she is for others*.
And while she always accused me
of never listening like the others,
I treated her in a way no other will,
no matter how spiritual.
Like Paul, *the more Christian than Christian*
(the Christ of the Church, in this case, *as social
economy*,
instead of a gathering
before which world *lets itself be seduced*),
I love her in potential, never loving her power—
my love always in a future that *does not exist*
but already moves (touches) the present.
I love her for *what she is and what she is not*.
I have always treated her as an equal—
never as a guru or a queen or a star—
and I never inflated *her existence*,
that residual fodder for the trappings of identity,
itself always subject to the Code.

110. What the poet keeps to himself

"*Let* my language be destroyed."

111. The non-linear love with narratives within its narrative

Rachel to my Ross, Cassandra to my Wayne
who says she loves me *in spite of* the pain,
that if she didn't love me I wouldn't be here,
who with her lack of clarity is being perfectly clear.

At the place where we can root each other on
that you undersold me with the surplus of the pawn,
trying to find a safe place for the vassal to land,
maybe you phase me out slowly with sweet reprimands.

Always competently assuring I'll be fine,
as my established strife has never been in decline,
you hover closely to the landing pad
for me to *jump off* w/o strength, with nothing to add.

And you'll find a pilot with a soft, safe voice
who lands the plane gently by removing his will
and letting the plane absently land without choice.
He'll take you from me daftly with his ghostly chill.

For what makes me most alive takes the best from me
that befriends me healthily indefinitely
and yet crushes me with each loving wince,
to return to grasp me when I'm no longer convinced.

And yet *what I say—is*! My life a spoken feat
that wins over the future with a cunning retreat,
one that *dashes* to get *its own fruits that it wants*,

whose linear breaks chime as a giant ducks the sconce.

Thus I will it shall be what helps my willing unwind
that, *in passing*, from the enigma won't lose sight
of its unlikely goal by giving its one of a kind—
and might *my actions* turn the destitute world's night.

The opportunity of the challenge is your greatest gift,
that *to prove* its merits, must be distant, not swift—
having in our love the luck of an opened cleft,
this hesitant self *realizes* a formerly *apparent* depth.

112. Past is Past. Present is Future.

The women are disappearing all at once.
Everywhere your silhouette the concave chalice hid
that I before ignored the double image in
and only saw the grail, a self-assertive dunce.

Like Jesus leaving us alone to ourselves *to bless us*
but to brutally never return to thus inflate his value,
we will the mercy of his cruel charitable '*to whom*',
like my life sentence for a criminalized momentary mess
up.

You are busy, busy, busy and I've too much time,
that my critical leisure turns its unlikely blind eye
toward your drift in space to a little choking dot.
As I mourn, you've the only tank the use of which *I*
taught.

When you were motionless and we ran into each other,
my decadent velocity sent you independently adrift.
I incautiously got everything I compassionately wished

and I watched you disappear slowly as I mutter

"Not again, not again, not again, not again"
at the summit of immoral convalescent values.
And I wish for your propulsion to never *have to*
but to recriminate willfully when you're out of my pin.

If I never do get another charitable chance
to go out seeking *someone* and yet with *you*, dance,
something I always wanted someone with whom to do,
untethered to the station, I'll swim the void ahead of you

and *on your trajectory*, you'll return to the first and last
me
with all that space between us having set you free
and with existential, everyday thinking you finally
decide
to *realize* your feelings and thus by them, no longer
abide.

113. Keep doing you, and I will endure

From the trembling I feel at mortality,
I shyly and wholly cherish our moments
that may become ever fewer in actuality
as you retreat into your wisdom, clever hermit.

They say you either live love or live fear,
but for me, each flows into the other—
that I feel powerful on the grate of the gutter
as you pull away and leave me here.

As a child, like a girl I dreamed of love,
what I never thought myself above—

and yet always find myself sadly below,
an illegal immigrant they have to stow.

I know you're perfectly well, I don't resent that,
and I know your appetite won't make you fat
from all the praise and power you receive,
and I'm thankful you don't yearn as much as me.

But the severance could also be momentary,
infinitesimally smaller than the until death,
or maybe you don't have any love left,
and I've to lie to myself, suppress my caring.

Still, I can see it in your eyes
and hear it in your cheerful replies
and feel it in these clutching hugs
or maybe you're still pulling out the rug.

Sometimes I do wonder if there's another,
sometimes I wonder if on the phone it's your brother,
sometimes I cry out in the night—
but I think it brave to risk these private frights.

But I'm quite sure any brief fling
couldn't spur what the magician brings—
who isn't here a master of illusions
that inevitably leads to your confusion.

And where the horror really chokes
is that to anyone you would have spoke
and treated the exact same as me
because you approach *every* person kindly.

And like many of them, I receive it as a flirt
and when I realize it's just kindness I am hurt,
but I only want this pain for myself

because I want you to focus on your health.

114. Real e-state

You're a lush field
going to waste conspicuously
behind a gaping barbed-wire fence.

As your value appreciates,
you're holding out for the best offer,
seducing offers with your obliging deterrents
and obvious removal from circulation.
One will eventually come in
and concrete over your ancient shape
for temporary gain
and permanent loss for you.

Once the strip malls of demand
you tease them to conceal you with
are all abandoned,
no one will remember that spacious clearing
behind that fence that deterred openly
honestly
and hysterically.

As you know, the best offer doesn't come
from the most interested
or whoever has the best development plans.

Nature's purity presents itself as garrulous artifice.
The concrete makes Nature seem a nostalgic simulation.

115. 10 Suggestions for Future Writers (Or What Has Worked
     for Me Thus Far)

  1. If you are sensitive like I was, when you're writing, stop
     reading; it is difficult if not impossible to say what you
     have to say and what someone else has to say. Not to
     mention, former heroes (like the parents) take their
     revenge in the twenties, when the neuroses establish
     themselves with greater sophistication *in the overcoming*
     of youth. Show your gratitude by not repeating.
     Creativity must need what no other creative has been
     able to satisfy. Thus, creativity is not free—it becomes
     free by doing the impossible (whatever is beyond the
     guarantees of easy solutions). You are the writer now.
     Bukowski, Baudelaire, Rimbaud, Bataille, Mallarme,
     Yeats—they are your enemies now. Leave them like old
     friends, about whom you think, perhaps wonder, but
     who you never miss. Of course, there is no good reason
     not to return to them once you have established a
     friendly distance from their influence, if only to better
     understand what to abandon and what to keep.
  2. Phenomenology, existentialism, surrealism, Dadaism,
     postmodernism, punk—these disciplines are dead. Give
     them up or perpetuate the status quo *that presents itself
     as the end of the status quo*. The current alternative is
     already a trap. The bourgeoisie is known not for
     innovation but for reverse engineering what exists and
     streamlining it (improving its minutiae). Do not lament
     the dissolution of what, anyway, was only *an attempt*.
  3. Don't trust the concepts "say everything" or "radical
     critique" or "pure negativity" or "genius," but don't
     completely deny the possibility that they may or may not
     have existed.
  4. Writing—like every art form—is an activity, not a
     lifestyle. If you reduce the whole to the part, both levels
     suffer—perhaps meeting each other half-way, where the

contented bourgeois resides. Sure, other people write, and you write also—there may or may not be 'a community of writers'. Still, limit yourself in content, not in form. Twitter expresses perfectly well—like the French poetry establishment did for Rimbaud—how platitudinous "writers" become in their obsessive-compulsive fixation, whereby they become mere servo-mechanisms of an exercise that is comfortably compatible with the oppressive demand to produce.

5. Write neither from the perspective of the last man nor that of the first (and thus self-made) man, but don't pretend to be oblivious either. The world-historical individual is almost never conscious of himself, but he acts out of necessity and, in the best cases, understands himself as such. As state above (1), it is absurd to try to create both a world and its double.

6. Write intermittently—in various places, at various times, in various moods. You are not subject to the imposed time. Graduate college in seven years, not four. Hold off on supporting yourself with a career that can 'pay for the rich experiences' necessary for the writer. If you are a great writer, the banal experience will be rich *in its banality*. Not to mention, the rich writer often forgets some of his 'best' ideas—and without too much of a fuss. The computer dies before something is saved. The drugs take their toll on the memory. That's ok because other ideas will come—some of them from the compost of dead ideas. Never write when or where or about what they expect you to. Become a morning person, make your bed, brush your teeth and write. If you consider yourself an intellectual, write in front of the TV, and sit in front of the TV for hours with nothing but trash on. If you're an Atheist, go to church, sing the hymns, smell the old people and write. If you're a communist, get a marking job and write. Apply for The Bachelor. Write at the dinner table with your grandparents. Write in parking

lots, dope holes and super-malls. There is nothing, no environment, no programming too offensive to invoke.

7. Feel free to change your mind. (Cf. Ecclesiastes) Writers often cling to depth. It ironically only makes them reflect a culture of repression, that even in its pornographic telescoping of the conditions of everyday life, never admits of its errors. They ignore their illusions, their relation to those illusions, and almost always claim authenticity. Inevitably, they remain middle-men.

8. Avoid expedients. These include narcotics, the so-called *festive attitude*, transcendental meditation, the city, bohemia, coffee, promiscuity, linguistics, travelling, mountaineering, etc. There is no substitution for the perspective. Entire industries are devoted to content-generation, the global tourism racket notwithstanding. The "prolonged derangement of the senses" is, at this stage (at which the world itself is a muralized distractionscape), counter-revolutionary.

9. Avoid the 'signs of being a writer'. Writers have historically just been unbridled individuals whose neuroses have been mistaken by those without an understanding of psychology for other-worldly powers. These writers have mystified others by mystifying themselves with signs that validate their continuity or success. Book shelves, record collections, urban art, cigarettes, typewriters, dope, unkempt apartments, obscure interviews, cities, collectives—these ready-mades are no longer trustworthy for qualifying a writer worth reading.

10. Assume and do not worry that whatever you write will be co-opted by whatever ideology supports and sustains the readers, for they are not *your* readers. In 2017, it doesn't seem likely that this tendency will disappear any time soon. History teaches that it is sometimes wise to expedite the madness of these imbeciles. For your secret teachings to become sweet to future free spirits, they

must likewise become bitter to the fettered spirits (even if they have no taste whatsoever for the great majority). This I owe to Nietzsche, who *explicitly* set traps for these types of reader who invariably continued down the path of decadence by making him *an authority* (or, if you prefer, a guru). Most have not learned how to read well, and are bad writers because of it.

The End

www.ingramcontent.com/pod-product-compliance
Lightning Source LLC
Chambersburg PA
CBHW060948050426
42337CB00052B/1813